# A WORLD BEYOND...

... is a totally unique exploration of the nature of man, God, and the universe—an answer to man's most disturbing and vital questions from a new prophet whose voice *will* be heard.

Fawcett Crest Books
by Ruth Montgomery:

HERE AND HEREAFTER

A WORLD BEYOND

# A WORLD BEYOND

A startling message from
the eminent psychic
Arthur Ford from beyond
the grave

## by Ruth Montgomery

A FAWCETT CREST BOOK

Fawcett Publications, Inc., Greenwich, Conn.

To RHODA MONTGOMERY,
who introduced me to
the exciting realm of
psychic phenomena

*A WORLD BEYOND*

THIS BOOK CONTAINS THE COMPLETE TEXT OF THE
ORIGINAL HARDCOVER EDITION.

A Fawcett Crest Book reprinted by arrangement with Coward,
McCann & Geoghegan, Inc.

Library of Congress Catalog Card Number: 77-154779

Selection of the Universe Book Club, October 1972

Printed in the United States of America
November 1972

# Foreword

Automatic writing is as mysterious as the cycle of birth and death and considerably more difficult to prove. We see a newborn baby and know that it has emerged from its mother's womb. We witness death and are aware that the life force has departed. Nothing remains but an outworn husk, which is cremated or sealed in a tomb. Automatic writing can also be seen, and even read, but the source of its intelligence and the propellant which directs the pencil or typing keys is unperceivable by any of our five physical senses. We know that many books have been written totally by means of this directed force, including the Patience Worth series received by a Midwestern housewife and the fascinating New Testament stories dictated through Geraldine Cummins.

Almost invariably the source claims to be a discarnate who once lived in the flesh, even as you and I. Some of those who doubt the existence of communication between the living and dead argue that the thoughts originate within the subconscious, where our memory bank is stored. Others believe that the messages are imparted by a superconscious, or higher, self which has contact with all knowledge through a sort of all-pervading ESP.

I don't claim to know the answer. I can only attest that the vivid descriptions of afterlife imparted through this book are not products of my imagination or conscious knowledge and that in those instances where assertions are provable, they were totally unknown to me before they came through my typewriter. Here is a case in point:

Dr. I. C. Sharma, head of the department of philosophy at Udaipur University, wrote an airmail letter to me from Udaipur, Rajasthan, India, on March 28, 1971. In this letter he said that he and his wife, Bhag, "had to leave Udaipur suddenly on account of the sudden death of my mother-in-law, Seeta Devi Manuja, who died at Hissar in India," and that they had just returned from the funeral. Knowing that I received automatic writing, he asked if I would try to receive some message that would comfort "dear Bhag."

The morning after Dr. Sharma's letter arrived in Cuernavaca, I asked Arthur Ford if he could give me any information concerning this deceased person, about whom I knew absolutely nothing, and he replied through automatic writing, "We have met and talked to Seeta, who is a lovely soul, bustling with energy and happiness to be here in this beautiful majesty. She loves her family and will not miss them, because she will be with them a great part of the time until they adjust to her physical absence." After several other personal comments about her, Ford wrote, "She asks that they remember a little blue flower that she particularly liked and to think of her when they see it, for she will be there too. Seeta, Seeta, Seeta. She is very like her name, which means 'flower of heavenly wonder' in this place of enduring life."

I had never before heard the name Seeta. I did not know if blue flowers even bloom in such a place as Hissar, which I had not known existed. I knew nothing about the interests of Mrs. Sharma's mother and therefore felt reluctant to transmit such a message to the head of a philosophy department in a faraway land, but I finally did so.

Under date of April 29, 1971, Dr. Sharma wrote again from Jodhpur, where he was assisting with university examinations. "Every word of the communication by Arthur Ford was correct," he wrote. "The blue flower was not known to me. But [my father-in-law] told me that during the last six months of Seeta's stay in the world, she had taken a fancy to flowers, particularly some blue flowers that grow in their courtyard, which she cultivated and used to decorate the living room with them. So her reference to liking the small blue flower was revealing for dear Bhag. It has given her great consolation."

Inasmuch as neither Dr. Sharma nor his wife knew of Seeta's recently developed interest in blue flowers until they checked after receiving my letter, and I had been unaware that Mrs. Sharma's parents were still living until his letter reported Seeta's death, I could not have gleaned this information through any normal type of mind communication. Surely the more rational explanation would be that Arthur Ford had contacted Seeta on "the other side" and had passed along a particular piece of information which would seem evidential to her daughter and son-in-law.

This book I believe to be Arthur Ford's own account of life in the next stages of existence beyond the portal that man calls death.

# I

# Arthur Ford Lives

The strident ring of the telephone roused me to reluctant consciousness. Wrong number, I decided drowsily, on noting that dawn was just beginning to break. I snuggled more deeply into the pillow, seeking to recapture an elusive dream, but the phone continued its shrieking protest, and at last I clutched for its raucous throat. A familiar voice at the other end of the international hookup said, "Ruth, this is Marianne Wolf in Philadelphia."

"Arthur is dead," I thought dully, and even as my heart turned to lead, Marianne continued. "I'm sorry to awaken you so early, but I wanted you to know before hearing it on the radio. Arthur Ford passed on early this morning in Miami."

Arthur Ford dead! It was too soul-shattering to contemplate. At that moment the top memo on my desk read, "Write Arthur." The day before I had tried to telephone him, only to find that I had misplaced the unlisted number of his new house in Florida. Two months earlier, while on a promotional TV tour for my latest book, I returned to the hotel in New York City to find a message, "Call Arthur Ford, not matter how late the hour." It was then nearly midnight, but I called him in Miami and we had a wonderful visit together. He had heard reports of my speech the evening before at New York's Universalist

Church and was pleased that I had highly praised him. He was feeling well and planning a lecture tour. It was the last time that I would hear his voice.

And now, a world without Arthur. It was January 4, 1971, and throughout that long day I mourned his passing. I remembered how much he had wanted to move with us to Cuernavaca, Mexico, when Bob and I decided to do so in 1969. Much as we would have loved to have him as a neighbor, we advised against it. The mile-high altitude might have an adverse effect on his heart, and the nearest hospital was fifty miles away in Mexico City. He therefore settled in Miami, to be near the heart clinic where he so often needed treatment. Now he would suffer no more from the excruciating attacks of angina pectoris, but selfishly I wanted him back. I had loved him as a father for a dozen years, and it was through Arthur's trance sittings that I first seemed to recapture the closeness with my own father, when he made his appearance through Fletcher, Ford's otherworld control.

Soon after meeting Arthur Ford I discovered that I was able to do automatic writing, and a high-minded control who called himself Lily dictated much of the material which I used in my book *A Search for the Truth* and in a chapter of *Here and Hereafter*. Then, after completing those two manuscripts, I abandoned automatic writing. For one thing, I was too busy. For another, I had proven at least to my own satisfaction that communication with the so-called dead is possible, and I had no wish to become a medium. I therefore shifted to more normal pursuits and wrote *Hail to the Chiefs: My Life and Times with Six Presidents,* which recounted my experiences as a syndicated Washington columnist. Now I was working on another book about the Mexican conquest, starring Malinche, the Indian princess who served as interpreter for Hernando Cortés. My family was breathing easily again. Ruth had abandoned the occult.

Late in that heavy-hearted January day after the telephone call, I suddenly felt an impelling urge to go to my

9

typewriter and once again try automatic writing. Probably nothing would occur, for I had deserted Lily so abruptly that there was no reason to expect such a busy spirit still to be on tap. But he was! No sooner had I murmured my usual prayer for protection and placed my fingers in touch-typing position than the writing began:

"Ruth, this is Lily and the group. Arthur Ford is here and wants you to know that he is as young as the merry month of May. He feels great and does not want you to grieve. He is so glad to be here, more delighted than you will ever know, for he has secretly yearned to make this trip of exploration and finds it much more beautiful than he had imagined or glimpsed while in trance. He's on top of the world. A ball of fire! He's so glad to be rid of the wornout body which caused him such pain."

As abruptly as it had descended on me that morning, the weight lifted from my heart. The next morning Lily presented my father, Ira Whitmer Shick, who wrote, "Ruth, Arthur and I are buddies now. He is a wonderful fellow and I appreciate all that he did to awaken you to this perfectly normal means of communication, but he says I should have some of the credit because you wanted to reach me enough to keep plodding away at it."

Arthur then came through himself, writing, "Ruth, this is Art. For the time being, never mind telling people that we're in communication, because every Tom, Dick, and Harry in the country is going to be claiming that, and I don't have time to answer all of their pleas for admission and response. Never was able to keep up with my correspondence anyway. Tell Marianne 'hi' for me and say how much I appreciate her taking the time to call you in my behalf. Wouldn't want to have shuffled off that mortal coil without my good friend Ruth knowing about it pronto, and Marianne likewise. You girls are very dear to me, and I'm appreciative of all that both of you did for me while there. Well, no good-byes are necessary because here I am, as you can see. I haven't gone anywhere. I like your Dad and expect to see plenty more of him in the weeks and months ahead. This is all for now, Ruth. Your friend, Art."

The next morning, with the urging of Lily, I agreed to resume the regular morning sittings at my typewriter, as I had done while amassing the material for *A Search for the Truth*. Lily then wrote, "Arthur is not here just now, as he wants to check on his funeral details and what to do with the estate that he left. But this is a passing phase, as he will soon learn that it makes no difference here what is done with what, and who is where." Lily gave me a sprightly report on my Aunt Mabel Judy, who had recently passed to the other side and was joyfully greeting old friends. Then Arthur bustled in and wrote in part, "This Lily is quite a guy. I sort of sensed his presence sometimes after I knew you in your plane, but he's a brilliant white light of radiant power and a mighty good influence to have on your side, so don't ever neglect him or fail to take advantage of his help."

Arthur immediately took an interest in my manuscript about Malinche, but only to the extent that he wanted me to hurry and finish it. Within a few days his reason became apparent. He wished me to be free to write a book in collaboration with him about life in the next stage of eternal life. With his usual zest, he assured me that he was collecting ample material, so that we could present "a totally accurate picture" of conditions in the plane where he now found himself.

On January 19 I received word from my editor in New York that another publishing house was advertising a book on Malinche, to appear in March. The coincidence was disconcerting, and because two books on the same subject within a year would be one too many, I dolefully packed away my half-finished manuscript. Lily and Arthur were delighted. The next morning Lily wrote, "We did not know of the other book until the news reached you personally. We are not all-seeing, all-knowing on this side, and many things are unknown to us on the physical plane unless they penetrate the intelligence of one with whom

11

we work closely, such as yourself. We wish to offer you our sympathy, but we personally are not sad about the news, for that manuscript was unnecessarily delaying our work together on a far more important and lasting project, that which Arthur Ford has been discussing with you. We will begin at once, if you are agreeable, and will delve into the existence of life from one stage to another, telling how it differs with each stage. We will discuss the crossover to this phase as one sheds his mortal body, and as we progress with our account of life here, I will give you glimpses of the higher phases which are yet to come."

I could scarcely wait, so I gladly followed Lily's instruction to put a clean sheet of paper in the typewriter. Arthur Ford then took over the typing with these words, "Ruth, you and I were together in many previous lifetimes, as I sensed there on your plane and now know to be a fact. We were friends and comrades, relatives in some lives and not in others, but never were we rivals or enemies, which is why we worked so well together and felt such consummate loyalty to each other in the phase which I have just finished. So much for a preface. Now, let us start with the premise that each person is a continuing entity through all eternity. No beginning and no ending, despite what some of the moralists say about our life beginning with physical birth as a baby and ending with Judgment Day. Bosh! There has never been a time when we were not, and we always will be, even though in constantly changing forms and stages, for we are as much God as God is a part of us. This will startle some, but not others. But what an expansive thought! For if each of us is God, then taken together we are God; and since it takes all of us to make a complete God, we know that another person is as necessary to us and to the common welfare as we ourselves. Therefore, it behooves each of us to concern ourselves mightily with others, for they are as necessary to us as our own arms and legs and eyes and ears.

"Each of us is incomplete without the totality of hu-

12

manity, both living and dead. Don't forget that this all-for-one-and-one-for-all applies equally to the living and so-called dead, for it is the totality that makes us the whole of the Universal Spirit which we are wont to call God. The clergy may not like this concept, but if you think about it awhile you realize that it is much nearer to fulfilling Christ's commandment 'Love One Another,' and His teaching that 'The Kingdom of God is within' than all the stuffy preaching about a God who sits on high to judge the quick and the dead. We are all a part of that Godhead."

Arthur would return to this philosophy again and again in the weeks ahead, expanding his thesis and making clear exactly what he meant, but at this point I was particularly interested in hearing about his reunion with Fletcher. As all who are familiar with Ford are aware, Fletcher was his French-Canadian boyhood friend in Florida who lost his life in World War I and a few years thereafter became the master of ceremonies for spirit entities who wanted to come through Ford while he was in trance. Arthur apparently sensed my curiosity, because the next morning he greeted me with, "Hi, Ruth. As I glanced around me on arriving at this stage I beheld my mother, my sister, and several other immediate members of the family, which made rejoicing easy. Then came Fletcher, whose ethereal face lit up like a dazzling aura to know that I had safely made the crossover without loss of realization and was now ready to release him from the task which he had often found onerous but was committed to fulfill.

"Fletcher's first words to me were, 'Old friend, welcome, welcome. And how happy is the release for both of us. Now I can go on to higher duties.' But first he talked to me at length, filling me in on what to expect on this side and giving me a few valuable words of advice about not becoming as earthbound as he did through taking over that long, drawn-out (fifty-year) project with me. That is why all of us are anxious for you, Ruth, to get on with this book. By taking on a short-term project like this one, I will be able to wrap up my earthly duties left undone, make a lasting contribution to the knowledge of all those good folks who looked to me for leadership in this field, and then go on to other duties here. I am not going to tie myself down to years and years of being a message bearer, as poor Fletcher did for me. Well, enough on that subject.

"Now let's get on with what life is like here in this stage of development. Understand that I'm new at this now, so will merely fill in what I have experienced to date, and will then take you along as I begin to grow on this side, so that the readers of our book will feel that they are experiencing it too. As to all that business about sidereal time versus orthic time, I'll leave that to the great brains like Betty and Stewart Edward White [authors of *The Unobstructed Universe*], who are quite advanced here, incidentally. Let's keep ours in layman's language that is easy of comprehension, so that we don't lose our readers in high-flown terms. Time, of course, *is* different. There's no such thing as clock time here, for we are able to eliminate time as well as space, since we are able to will ourselves to be anywhere at any moment of earth time and are able to look ahead so far into what you call the future that this also transcends the earthly idea of time. For things *are* planned ahead—make no mistake. If earthlings realized how much of it is planned ahead, they would not struggle so strongly to avert certain catastrophies, as they view them, because why worry so much when it's all laid out in front of you anyway? Just accept as it comes, remembering always to do the very best that you can to lead productive, helpful lives, and let the future come to you unfeared; for whether it's part of the divine plan for you or your own mission which you agreed to accomplish when you returned to physical form, it's there. So what is fear? Simply lack of faith in the plan. Be relaxed, available, willing to take what comes and do the best that you can."

The following day Arthur lifted the curtain a little

higher on his initial reception in the spirit world, writing, "Death is no more than the passage through a beckoning door. It is so brief, so transitory as scarcely to be noted, for it is what lies beyond the door that counts. The body, let us say, is tired and weakened. At a certain point the heart stops, not merely because the body mechanism will not function, but also because the soul has slipped off through the opening door. Some go gladly, some reluctantly, but all in answer to the universal urge for peace and tranquility.

"For a time the soul in transit may slumber, particularly if there has been undue shock or mental weakening. On this side they let it sleep until it stirs and seems to feel need, of its own accord, for contact with those on this side. But sometimes the step across is so gentle as to seem like the wafting of a summer's breeze. This was so in my case, because I knew enough of what to expect to welcome the shedding of the husk which was my ailing body. The pain ceased, the spirit departed, and here I was amid such beauty as you cannot dream. The *here* was not different from the *there* except that, with no need for physical comforts, only the beauty of the world remained.

"I found that it was as I subconsciously remembered, although no one can quite recall the beauty and the deep affinity that one has for others of like-thinking here. It was like coming home, to slip through that door and release the tired old body. In an instant, without conscious thought, I was here surrounded by relatives, and my mother was saying, 'Hallelujah, Arthur. Welcome to Canaan Land.' Well, it isn't Canaan Land, but my mother was of the small-town evangelical pattern, and to her it still seems like it, because that is what she expected to find here.

"Let's clear out the minds of those on your side who cling to those childish patterns of imaginative thought. It retards their progress here to expect such nonsensical things. Instead of clothing the truth with so much fluff,

15

which takes time to strip away, it would be better to proceed with the work at hand. There is work here, but only that which is purposeful, necessary, and congenial. No one is forced to work at any task. He himself chooses what to do, and if it helps with his spiritual growth, that is enough to make the angels sing, as the preachers say. But he will never be compelled to grow or develop. No teachers on this side to force Johnny to learn to read or spell, unless Johnny wants to grow and develop. Therefore we need to be stronger here than there. Understand? There we are pushed against our will by loving parents and teachers to make something of ourselves. Here we're left to our own devices, and the lazy ones loaf by the wayside, without ever putting their feet upon the path and searching for the Way.

"At least that's what I've found to date, although admittedly I'm a newcomer in a land that is never the same to a soul, even though we pass along this way after each earthly incarnation. We are different each time we come through the open door again. We have formed new patterns of thought and new ideas about what to expect, and since thoughts are definitely things, we are the cocreators with God of what we find for ourselves here. Ruth, we want you to wake up the people there to the importance of this towering truth. They, with their thoughts, are not only creating the pattern of their future lives but their own heaven or hell."

As if to illustrate his point, Arthur referred to my Aunt Mabel, who had crossed to the other side about the same time that he did. A spinster schoolteacher throughout most of her long life, she was the soul of generosity, and we loved her dearly. But like my mother, who shared her small town Midwestern background, she lamented my interest in psychic phenomena. Arthur, in his report on Aunt Mabel, declared, "At first she joyously greeted old friends and relatives, rushing from one to another. But then I noted a change. On your side she was narrow-minded, devout, and good, but she had no original thoughts and

16

was too circumspect to seek them. Here she is even more so, for this plane goes against what she had been led to expect of a heaven, and thus she sometimes feels that she is in the wrong place. There is no such thing as a right and wrong place. It is all one, one with you there and with us here, but what we make of it here is influenced by what we had expected while on your side.

"Since Mabel expected harps and angels floating amid palaces and sylvan glens, she is for a time disappointed. But that will pass as she develops, provided that she works at it. Otherwise, a soul can remain in a kind of suspension for many thousands of years. Growth. Growth of spirit as well as development of soul are essential whether here or there. We are the ones who must put forth the effort to grow. Nothing will grow in our behalf. That is why I would have you picture each of us as God, as well as a part of God, for you and we are the gods who decide whether we grow or remain as embryos.

"Progression. That is the key to happiness here as well as there, and what an exciting place this is for those of us who are eager to learn and to grow. We have sky and flowers, trees, sunsets more vivid than you can comprehend; for everything in this world and in yours is a pattern of thought. Here we communicate and work and grow and thrive only through thought, and since we are without interference from physical minds, which are mere mechanical machines, our thoughts instantaneously react to whatever we wish to project. We instantly see another person or soul of whom we think. We are constantly projecting thought patterns of our own, so that wherever we wish to be, we are.

"We are unaware of the filth, the degrading slums, the polluted air, because we do not respond to them except as half-forgotten ideas. Thoughts are things, you know, and into our thoughts we are able to put whatever we choose to see, just as you in physical bodies are able to make your lives sweeter or uglier by what you think. Think evil and evil comes, think goodness and you see

17

only goodness in those about you. Think love and you are surrounded by love, think hate and the world is a loathsome place filled with ogres and baneful voices. Thus, we in the spirit soon learn better than to think degrading thoughts. Our minds, which are actually spirit, project their own thought patterns, so that it is easy to recognize those of like thought patterns, and we find each other. As we used to say, 'Birds of a feather flock together,' or 'Like begets like.' Who would want to be in a slum alley or at a crowded Coney Island-type resort, when the mere thought of windswept beaches bright with sun or mountain hideaways with monumental views are available for the thinking?"

During my last telephone conversation with Arthur Ford, I had suggested that he write another book about the psychic for my editor, Ellis Amburn, and he had promised to consider it. Now he broke into his discussion of the next world to say, "Tell Amburn that this should more than compensate for the book that I was not able to write for him there. There was little new I could have added to what I had already written from that side, but now we will be able to reveal many of the things which have long puzzled mankind on that side of the door. Lily and his group want me to tell you all that we can about the state of being on this side, the whys and wherefores which make it important to prepare there for this side, the purposes of meditation and prayer, the interlocking relationship between the two, and the way of life on this side. We hope by so doing to awaken thoughtful, thinking people to the reality that each day there is wasted unless some progress has been made in preparing for the steps ahead.

"Take a youngster's school books, for instance. Each day he prepares a new lesson, more advanced than the day before, progressing through many lessons until examination day, when the teacher grades him on his progress. Simple, isn't it? Easy to understand. All right, view life in the physical body the same way. We all come back there to go to school and learn how to grow and develop more speedily, as well as to test ourselves on the progress made on this side. In the spiritual sense it is like the little child at school. Each day offers new challenges, new opportunities, new ways to test soul development and inner growth. Each day lost from meditation is a day wasted, and the time runs out rapidly for all of us. If people could see what I see from this side, they would realize that each lifetime is little more than a flash of lightning in duration, and the eons which sometimes occur between earth lives are slow waiting periods, unless we're doing some extraordinary work like Lily here, or Fletcher, or the ones who worked through Eileen Garrett [a famous Irish-American psychic known personally to Arthur and me], and others to try to bring the message to those who will open their minds in your phase."

He interrupted himself to add, "By the way, I've seen Eileen several times here. No more arthritic pains or emotional upsets; calm, serene, beautiful, fully awake now, as the veil drops when we cross through the door. She is keen to be on with her work, too, but wants to find just the right link that will carry on the research that she was doing there."

# II

# The Arthur Ford Saga

Arthur Ford was America's best-known living medium at the time that he suffered his fatal heart attack. Scholarly, well read, and urbane, with a pixie humor and wry wit, he was a delight to have around, whether conscious or in trance. Throughout the fifty years of his mediumship, he sat for the world's mighty and the humble nonentities with equal grace. He was totally without race prejudice, and although convalescing from a severe heart attack at the time, he joined other clergymen on the first March on Washington, which was led by Martin Luther King. Why? Because he believed in human rights.

He was an accomplished clairvoyant and an excellent psychometrist, but he was not a direct voice medium. In other words, he could seemingly pick up messages from the deceased, even when fully awake, and he could discern a great deal about an absent person simply by handling some object that had belonged to him; but when in trance, it was Fletcher who conveyed messages from the so-called dead. The discarnates did not speak directly through Ford by trumpet. Thus, he was able to operate at all times in full light, by simply tying a dark handkerchief across his eyes to facilitate his own trance sleep.

Those who call themselves direct voice mediums insist upon total darkness, arguing that trumpets cannot float in the light, and they may be correct. Unfortunately, however, such blackened rooms provide cover for hocus-pocus if the medium is so inclined; whereas with Ford it was always possible to take copious notes or tape-record the proceedings.

Ford was a modest, unassuming man who sometimes regarded his unique gifts as a heavy cross to bear, but because he also came to regard mediumship as his mission in this particular lifetime, I never heard him complain. As a boy in Titusville, Florida, his family's entire social life centered around the church. His mother's family had been staunch Southern Baptists for many generations, and because Arthur devotedly attended every morning and evening service and was active in the young people's Union, his mother assumed that he would become a Baptist minister. Arthur's mother remained a Baptist until her death, but her son developed such iconoclastic views after reading tracts of the Unitarian Church that the local Baptists read him out of their parish. He won a scholarship to Transylvania University, and shortly after World War I was ordained a Christian minister in the Disciples of Christ Church. By then he had discovered his psychic talents, and the pulpit soon lost him to the world stage, although much of the remainder of his life was to be spent in awakening the minds of fellow clergymen to the vista of a continuing life which can be perceived beyond the five physical senses.

Arthur Ford was a ministerial student at Transylvania in Lexington, Kentucky, at the outbreak of World War I and after a ninety-day training course was commissioned a second lieutenant. Assigned to Camp Grant, he was a self-assured young officer until he awakened one morning "seeing" the names of those in camp who had died of influenza during the night. He told himself that he could shake off the disquieting dream by going over to see the real roster, but when he picked it up he discovered that not only were the names identical, but even in the exact order which he had "seen" them. For the next two mornings the phenomenon recurred, and when some of his buddies doubted his story, he told them the names that he saw as soon as he awakened. Again the camp roster confirmed his dream, and this time there were witnesses. Soon he began dreaming the names of those killed in the Rainbow Division fighting overseas, and the casualty lists in the daily newspaper invariably confirmed his dream roster in the same sequence.

With the end of the war he returned to Transylvania, and to his immense relief the disturbing dreams ceased, for he feared insanity. Not until Professor Elmer Snoddy, a psychology instructor, introduced him to books on mysticism did he learn that many other people, including John Wesley, Martin Luther, Emanuel Swedenborg, Dwight Moody, and Catholic saints, had experienced psychic phenomena. This new knowledge eased his Puritan conscience, and with a small group of professors and clergymen, he began experimenting with table tipping and clairvoyance. His curiosity was so piqued that he made a summer trip to New York to inspect the work of the American Society for Psychical Research, and his interest in the occult continued after he became a full-time minister at a small parish in Barbourville, Kentucky. During his second year in that ministry he met Dr. Paul Pearson, founder-president of the Swarthmore Chautauqua Association, who persuaded Arthur to join his lecture circuit as a speaker on psychic subjects.

The young minister fully intended to return to the pulpit in the fall, but he never did. He studied for a time under Swami Yogananda, an Indian mystic who was then lecturing in the United States, and with the rapid development of his psychic powers he became a sensation in London as well as New York. In 1924 Fletcher assumed the task of acting as unseen interlocutor between the living and dead while Ford was in trance, and Sir Arthur Conan Doyle persuaded Arthur to become a professional medium. The author of the Sherlock Holmes books believed that both ministers and mediums are

22

"called of God," and since there were many more of the former than the latter, he argued that his young friend Art should choose mediumship.

In 1928 Ford broke the Houdini code which the deceased magician had managed to transmit through the unconscious Ford to his wife, Beatrice Houdini, and although carping critics shouted "fraud," Mrs. Houdini issued a written statement that only she and her late husband had known the agreed-upon code message that Ford transmitted.

Arthur Ford's trance performances were repeatedly tested by some of the best known personalities of the times: the great English physicist Sir Oliver Lodge; Professor William McDougall, of the psychology department at Harvard; novelists Upton Sinclair, Jack London, Gerald Heard, Hugh Walpole, and Sir Arthur Conan Doyle; Dr. Sherwood Eddy, world secretary of the Young Men's Christian Association; and many other writers, artists, Senators, Congressmen, White House intimates, and European nobility. He lectured on three continents and was at the peak of his amazing career when, en route from South Carolina to New York, his automobile was struck by a tobacco truck near the North Carolina line. His sister and a friend were killed in the accident, and Arthur was so near death from multiple internal injuries that a doctor kept him under heavy sedation to ease his final days. Unfortunately, the young physician was more interested in Arthur's psychic powers than in his physical welfare, and when he discovered that his drugged patient could diagnose the ailments of other patients in the small hospital, he continued the massive injections of morphine long after they were needed.

Arthur's dope addiction was finally discovered by another physician, who promptly removed him from the hospital to New York, but he suffered such agonies during the withdrawal phase that a doctor-friend suggested a shot of alcohol to steady his nerves and invite sleep. Ford had never before touched liquor, but he uncovered a remarkable capacity for it. Not until he had consumed more than a bottle of scotch did he at last feel its effects and fall asleep. For the next twenty years he fought tension with alcohol, as he continued to travel around the world and appear on lecture platforms, but now he was addicted to alcohol instead of morphine. He tried numerous cures, but nothing could break the habit, until in desperation he turned to Alcoholics Anonymous and began to find himself again. During those prolonged bouts with the bottle his psychic powers were not impaired, and he continued to bedazzle audiences here and abroad.

Despite his worldwide renown, I had never heard of Arthur Ford until 1956, when I began researching the subject of psychic phenomena at the Congressional Library for a series that I was to write for International News Service. Nearly every book had some favorable reference to medium Arthur Ford, and many of the authors described such evidential sittings with him that I was intrigued, although I was then a nonbeliever in communication between the living and dead. Several years later, when I learned that Ford was to deliver a lecture at a Swedenborgian church in Washington, I went to hear him and afterward made an appointment to interview him for my syndicated column.

The subject of our interview was a new organization called Spiritual Frontiers Fellowship which Ford and a group of other clergymen, college professors, and professional men had formed to probe psychic phenomena within the framework of existing churches. Before departing his hotel suite, I confessed that I had recently published a newspaper series debunking mediums, and he bravely volunteered to go into trance for me then and there. The impressive results of that seance have been previously recorded in my book *A Search for the Truth*.

I wrote an article about Ford's prowess, and thereafter he visited with us whenever he came to Washington. I often invited friends to sit in on Arthur's seances, and their identities were unknown to Ford. But not to Fletcher!

At each sitting he brought through a wealth of evidential material about them from deceased relatives, each of whom he identified by name. Throughout the ensuing years Arthur often stayed at our houses in Washington and Virginia Beach. He wrote frequent letters filled with dry wit, and we talked innumerable times by long-distance telephone. We shared lecture platforms and became such devoted friends that we were never out of touch for more than two or three weeks at a time. But not until Arthur passed through what he calls the open door did we have such regular communication as we now enjoy at the same hour each morning.

# III

# Thoughts Are Things

At one of our sessions shortly after Arthur Ford took over my typewriter, he wrote, "Ruth, today let's discuss what happens when a person like myself comes over here, happy to be rid of a fractious body and eager to continue the search for spiritual development. Let me say first of all that I knew what to expect, for often in my trance states I had glimpses of the people on this side and knew that they were as much with us on the earth as my friends there. They were eager to assist and happy to give me a rousing welcome, for they had seen me wandering on what we call the other side. Understand that I had no wish to hurry the coming state. I was willing to serve out my time in the body, and because I had often abused that body (with alcohol) it was not in as good a shape as if I had taken better care of it. That in itself is a lesson for those of you there. Don't abuse your body, for it is a temple of the living God, and the more we respect it and use it like a spirit temple, the better it will respond to our needs.

"Now, as the time approached for me to return here, where I had often been between previous lives, I felt a quickening of the spirit within me. I became more contemplative and tried to prepare my subconscious mind for the freedom which it would know when it became a free

26

spirit, for it is the one which comes with us and stays with us and is the mind of the spirit. For that reason, if for no other, it is good sense on that side of the so-called veil to let the subconscious develop along with the conscious mind. Give it freedom to expand and to demonstrate its remarkable powers, instead of keeping it under too tight a rein so that only the conscious mind rules the heart and head.

"All right. So at the end, after that final heart seizure, I keenly sensed that my time was at hand, and I will say emphatically that I longed for and then welcomed the release from physical restraints. As my spirit or soul left that wearied body, I stepped as easily into the astral body as if I had always consciously worn it. The lightness, the freedom from restraint, the heavenly elixir of being without the heavy flesh was beyond description. What a relief! How glorious to know that I was as much *here* as ever I had been, but without restraint, without barriers, without suffering. Gloriously free to move about at any time and any place without so much as a railroad ticket or a walking step. It was better than being an active boy again, for here there are no barriers, no barricades, no blocks to our free passage. The mind wills where we will be, and there we are. The net effect is to be as nearly Godlike as it is possible for mere souls to be.

"At first I was busy greeting friends on this side and looking up Fletcher, who was smilingly awaiting my greeting. What a noble soul he has become since I knew him as a boy! We have had wonderful sessions, and he still remembers you and all the help that you gave our work by your courage against odds to tell the world of this mission of his and mine. Well, he will rest now, for his mission is accomplished and he has the choice of going on to a much higher plane or returning to another earthly existence, and as yet he has not made his determination. But one thing is definite: He is not coming through to others there, and the mediums who claim that he is sending messages to them are full of hogwash, or worse.

27

Fletcher had always made it definite that when I came over he would be freed of the mission that he had set for himself."

Another day, as if to clarify the freedom that he now enjoys, Arthur wrote, "Life on this side is not too different from that on your plane, for we are *here*—not off in some other world. I am as much with you at this moment as ever I was when sitting in your living room in Washington, except that we now communicate more effectively. We are here! That is the first thing to emphasize. We are as much of the earth as you are, except that because we have shed the physical bodies, we are not tied to the basic laws which operate for you and provide impediments to movement. We are spirit and can go through inanimate objects—or animate, for that matter. They exist only as thought forms, and since we see them not so much as forms as ideas, they are no hindrance to us. We are able to live in houses of thought forms, or on sunny slopes beside streams, or wherever we like to think of ourselves as being. But they are totally nonessential, since we need no habitation. We are as free as the wind to go wherever we choose at any given moment, but this is not to say that we rush about willy-nilly, for we soon develop purpose here. Growth is what counts here as well as there, and we do not grow so long as we transport ourselves aimlessly hither and yon.

"Our purpose here is the same as there, to do that which God wishes for each of us. No two of us is alike, and our missions down through the ages have varied as much as the earthly personalities with which we drape our spirit. Here we do not actually see God, but we are so overwhelmingly aware of His beneficent presence that none on this side who has experienced the slightest bit of development will be unaware of His constant presence. We are His and He is ours. There is no separation from Him, for we are of Him. As easy to think of the finger of one hand going its separate way without command from the physical mind as to think of a soul as a separate

28

entity from God, the Creating Force. We are all one, you and I and our neighbors and enemies and our God. There is no division. There is no separation. We are as responsible for the salvation of our enemy as we are for our own, inasmuch as we are inseparable from him in the bosom of the Lord. When we speak of being cocreators with God, we mean that He is as much a part of us as are our toes and fingers."

Perhaps it is a hang-up from his ministerial days, but Arthur invariably waxes more eloquent about spiritual matters on the Sabbath. Early in our work together with the automatic writing, this truth became so apparent that on the first day of each week Lily would introduce him by dryly commenting, "And here's Art with his Sunday sermon."

Ford had been dead less than three weeks, when on January 24, 1971, he wrote, "Hi, Ruth. Happy Sunday! This, then, will be our day to discuss the more spiritual aspects of the life which lies ahead for all of you still on your side, which I must say I'm glad not to be a part of anymore. We will first consider the aspect of God, the one abiding force which melds all else together. This force or power is so intense that nothing will survive if it should fail for so much as the batting of an eye. It is the glue of the universe, the melding together, the complete atom. It is not, as some would have us think, a spirit but a force—a tremendous force for good that knows no other than good, for how could bad glue hold it all together? This force or Godhead is the universal truth, the universal good, the universal all-in-all. But there is room within the orb of this centrifugal force for disharmony and greed and evil. There is some evil in every living thing that falls into disharmony with the centrifugal force. The only remedy is to unite again in perfect harmony, for then there is no evil, no greed, no sickness, no disharmony. Time and again we come back here to learn that simple truth. Disharmony is the root of all our evils.

"Take a rose and examine it closely: leaves, stem, and

petals. Perfection, you say. But wait! Is there not something lacking? Perhaps one missing leaf, one petal curled a bit too much? So do you blame the flower, or the beetle, or the wind, or some other outside influence which affected its perfect symmetry? Something went awry, but what? God created the pattern which all roses were to follow. Therefore He will not be to blame if the pattern is sometimes faulted and error imposed against His wish. So it is with man. God, or this powerful force, if you prefer, gave the pattern for mankind. Each part fitted neatly into other parts, so that the whole was perfection. The first man to appear in flesh on this planet was perfection without blemish. Call him Adam or what you will, he was the creation of the central force that we call God. This man was a thought pattern transmitted by that centrifugal force, but with the advent of other humans, both male and female, strife arose—a warring of the spirits who had lived amicably together before flesh was inhabited by them but who now quarreled over portions of a land which was so blessed that everything was there in abundance for all to use and develop.

"This strife created ugly thought patterns, and since thoughts are things, errors began to appear in the framework of human beings missing toes, malformed heads, diseased minds, as these spirits continued to return to the flesh, until finally God sent again an example of perfect man in the one we call the Nazarene. Again the perfect being, the pattern without flaw, and some were wise enough to follow Him and worship the perfection of this son of God. Others, as you know, hooted derisively and sought to blot out this perfect pattern by their own lust and greed and evil ways. But we will continue to seek perfection so long as our souls seek the love of God. This is the glue that binds us all to this central force: the power of love. So love one another, love God, and love thyself. Attune yourself in harmony with this all-powerful force."

As the writing progressed from day to day, Arthur so

often referred to God as a force that I finally broke in to ask, "Who or what is God? Do you know more about Him now than when you were here in the flesh?"

"Much more, Ruth," he instantly replied. "God is the core of the universe from which all else flows forth. He is truth and energy. He is matter and spirit, and all things of heaven and earth. He is eternity itself, wise and all-knowing, but whether we are aware of it or not, He is also the essence of our being, without which nothing would exist. It is His total harmony which melds together the universe and all therein and thereon, so that without His perfect Being the universe would instantly fall apart. God is! The eternal I Am. He is so sublime that we are unable to grasp His full. Without God there is nothing and no thing. With Him there is truth and light and radiance and total harmony. He is life itself, and because this is true, there is no life or being without Him. Thus we are as much a part of Him as He is of us, and because we are imperfect in our reactions and behavioral pattern, we must strive ever onward through many earth cycles until we achieve sufficient perfection to rejoin God as co-creators. It is the law, for no imperfect thing will ever have the opportunity to become a part of the Godhead, which would not function properly if full of imperfections. It is the law, immutable. Thus our ceaseless attempts to return to the physical state in order to erase our rough edges and be able to fit into the Godhead as perfect segments of the whole."

Still puzzled, I commented, "This makes God sound like an impersonal force. Does He then hear our individual prayers?"

Arthur replied, "God is total awareness. He not only hears prayer but knows without being asked what the plea is going to be. He is truth supreme, wisdom all-knowing, and without Him there would be only chaotic blackness. He is light and truth and love. He is above all our Creator and our Father, who loves each and every one of us. This I know, and when we approach Him lovingly and trust-

31

ingly, as we would a wise parent, He is ready to grant that which is for our best interests if it harms no one else. Not all prayers are therefore granted, but only those which spring from a faithful and loving heart. He heals, He loves, He comforts. He watches over us night and day and at every season of the year. Ruth, God is All!"

The following morning, Arthur declared that he wanted to explain about the transition which occurs as a soul sleeps away and awakens in spirit form. "We are not speaking now, as we will later, about sudden or unexpected death," he wrote, "but of the natural transition of a soul who sheds a tired or ailing body. The soul slides easily from its casing without pain or visible sensation. One moment he is there, still wearing the painful garb of flesh, and the next he is in heavenly raiment. That is not as fanciful as it sounds, for this actually occurs if the transition has been prepared for. We awaken into a realm of pure beauty and song. The trees are *real* trees here, not the reflections which you in the flesh see. The flowers are pure thought form and therefore much more exquisite than anything actually in the form seen by physical man. The birds, animals, spirits, yes, the many mansions are perfection here, for they are thought forms.

"As we awaken here we see this enchantment at first as in a dream. Is it real? Is it conceivable? Well, not by man is it conceivable, but by the force of love. There is nothing we want that we cannot think into being at this point, except for another body of flesh, for this latter is not ours to command at any instant but a right to be earned either through long preparation and soul searching or because sudden death not of our making entitles us to a quick return to physical form, if we desire it. This we will discuss later in more depth.

"Let us assume, then, that we are tired of the old body and eager to get on with life in this great world. For a time we rest and enjoy reunion with old friends. Depending on the worth of our characters, we are troubled or at ease, happy or restless, just as on the earth plane.

32

Little by little, as we adjust to the sudden alteration in soul covering, we realize that time is passing swiftly, that we would be on with our Father's business, if you will. That is when our true character begins to assert itself. Will we want to plunge into a round of festivities and pure pleasures, or will we want to develop our spiritual side? And if we choose the latter, do we think of it in terms of self-growth and self-advancement or as group growth and development? That is to say, will we want it for others as much as for ourselves? Remember what I told you earlier. The race advances only as all of us surge upward toward the common goal of enlightenment and perfection. Therefore, if we would advance rapidly ourselves we must make the effort to see that others of like interest are also given every tool for self-advancement."

The next day he resumed where he had left off, writing, "Now if the soul should be tainted with horrendous sins against others (the only true sin) then that soul will lie fallow for a long time, unless it is so beset by evil that it returns to trouble those left behind. We do not call this 'haunting' over here, but 'persecution.' Sometimes the soul does not realize that he has passed into spirit, so he hovers around, wondering why no one seems to pay attention to him, on the physical plane. Other times he makes a deliberate return, unable to give up thoughts of worldly goods and possessions. These troubled souls cannot be helped by our work on this side as much as they can through prayer from those of you still in the physical state. Pray for them.

"Others who come over suddenly, through accidents or war, feel great shock on learning that they are in the spirit world and will no longer be able to earn money, play ball, or do the things to which they are accustomed. For us this task presents problems, because we will not at first be able to convince them that this is the heaven they had heard about as children. We try to tell them gradually, bit by bit, for they perceive that all is as it was there except for the vividness of the thought patterns, which makes everything glitter and gleam more brilliantly than they remembered.

"We welcome a newcomer with love and open arms. He is surprised at first, unless he has prepared for this step through study and meditation. He hungers and we produce food. It is a thought pattern, but as real to him as that which he once used to sustain his physical body. He thirsts, and we give him drink. He is gradually making the transition, and has not yet accustomed himself to the idea that he will no longer need food and drink. He asks about loved ones whom he does not see around him. Some are still in physical body, some here, some already progressed to a higher state or gone back into another earthly body. We tell him to wait, that within a short time he will understand more, and that meanwhile he is to do whatever suits his fancy. Some will explore the countryside, gasping in awe at the brilliant colors and lush foliage. Others may wish themselves in a big city and immediately will be there, soaking up the sounds and dodging traffic as excitedly as if they needed to do so. For a time we let them do exactly as they choose. It's up to them. But we are ever within call, and the day comes that they tire of this way and begin to wonder more about their present circumstances. If of a studious nature they will want to join classes, for we have them here. Others may join groups who are experimenting with earthly contact.

"But let's take a look at a specific case. A man coming here after a short but severe illness stirs, wakens, opens the eyes of his astral body, and sees a grassy plain with brook, trees, and forests beyond. It looks inviting, but he thinks that he is dreaming it because he recalls having been sick. He decides to take a few tentative steps in the direction of the stream and discovers that he moves effortlessly, without pain. Perhaps there is good fishing there. No one is in sight as he strolls along the grassy slope, and he wonders how a stream has managed to stay so glittering and unpolluted. The sparkling water ripples, and fish are joyously jumping in and out of the spray.

The man wishes that he had brought a fishing pole and instantly finds one in his hand. He casts and pulls in a beautiful sturgeon. He is elated and can scarcely wait to show the boys when he gets home. He continues to pull in whopping fish until the pastime dulls, because he realizes that he has more than he and his friends can consume. He wonders where he left his car, and it is then that he begins to realize that he is in strange territory. How did he get here? When did he come? It would be a dream except that he can touch and smell the fresh-caught fish—for our astral bodies possess all the senses of physical ones, and more besides.

"Well, what a predicament! The car is nowhere in sight, and he has seen no signs of human life. He ponders what to do next. Light is beginning to fade, or so he believes, and he wonders if his family will worry about him. Suddenly he wants terribly to be at home, and he is instantly in his hometown, watching strangers bending over his body. What are they doing? Giving him medicine, perhaps? But no. This is not a sickbed, but a morgue. Something must be terribly wrong. He rushes to his house and sees his wife wearing black. Voices are muted as people come and go. Some dire mistake has apparently been made, because they seem to be mourning him, when he is right there waiting to show them the best fish catch he ever made. His wife looks at him as he stands in the doorway and instead of speaking begins to cry. 'What's wrong, honey?' he asks, but no one seems to notice that he has spoken. 'Hey, what's up?' he finally demands, but silence greets his perfectly logical question.

"He strolls over to his wife, pulls her head against him, and asks, 'Why are you crying? I never felt better in my life, so dry your tears, and let's have fish for dinner.' She makes no reply. He is disconcerted. Why was everyone acting so strangely and refusing to speak to him? What has he done to offend these relatives and friends? He drops the fish and mopes at the kitchen table. When will all these people go home, so that his wife will come

35

and help him fix dinner? He wishes that the fish were already cleaned and scaled, and as he looks back at them he is surprised to see that they are all ready for the skillet. His wife must have slipped in and cleaned them while he was napping, although he was not conscious of having slept. But his wife does not come again, even though he opens the door and calls to her. He is desolate. That roomful of people, and no one paying the slightest attention to him or the fish. At this point he exclaims, 'I might as well be dead,' and as he mutters the slang expression he finds himself back on the grassy plain beside the brook. But this time there are other people there enjoying the scenery. Half afraid of being ignored as he was by his family, he murmurs a timid 'hello,' and instantly they surround him with the warmth of friendship. They ask him about his fishing catch, how he likes the view, and from whence he has come.

"He tells them that he has mislaid his car, and one of them remarks that he won't need it anymore, because he can will himself to any spot he wishes to go to. This so puzzles him that he falls into a deep stupor. When he finally rouses, the people have gone, all but one man with a long white beard who says, 'Son, time now for us to start to school.'

" 'School?' he exclaims. 'I finished school long ago, old man, and you must surely have done the same.'

" 'But a different kind of school, my lad,' the old man continues. 'This is the real school where we are taught how to remember, how to forget, and what to know without learning.'

"The man is deeply puzzled, but he follows the old man to a schoolhouse where several other strangers are seated in a classroom of sorts. One of them looks like a lawyer whom he knew in the Lions Club, but since he died a week or two ago, he must be mistaken. The class is called to order and the old man begins by saying, 'I presume that all of you know why you are here.' In the silence that follows, the newcomer raises his hand and says in a

36

loud voice, 'No, sir, I do not know. Why am I here?' The others turn to look at him, and in their eyes he reads understanding. They too have obviously wondered but must have learned the answer. The old man says slowly, 'Listen well, son, for this is one of the most important lessons you will ever learn. To those of you gathered here let me say that we welcome James as a newcomer to our land of spirit. He has not yet adjusted to the change, but because this same confusion has so recently been the lot of all of you, we will pitch in to help him over the rough spots. James, we are nearer to you than hands and feet, so in your perplexity you will never need to be alone. Simply accept for the time being that your family and friends will not be able to see and converse with you, even though you are able to see and talk with them. This proves that you are more alive than they are, because your faculties are so much greater now that you have left the body. But for the time being they will view you as nothing but thin air and think of you as beneath the ground. Such a pity . . . but that is where you will take up your lesson tomorrow.' "

Arthur Ford also stopped there, and the following day he digressed to say that this book was to be the story of the "actual passover of various types of souls from the physical life to the spirit." Then he continued, "Those who want mansions will find them ready, but those who want food for the spirit will find it in abundance, for that is what this is all about, material versus spiritual, and it is up to each soul to choose which way he will go.

"Now as to that fisherman yesterday. That was his hobby while in the flesh, and he had dreamed of making such a catch in some such beautiful spot before he came here. But he felt downcast when he discovered that there was no one to help him cook the fish and to talk it over with. Those in the flesh were not able to share his pleasure because they did not know he was there. After a time he began to realize that they would no longer be able to see him and that his new life was even more exacting than

37

the previous one, but with rules so firmly established that he had no reason to question them or to exert pressure against them. He is becoming well adjusted now and no longer hangs around his former house. He is learning that each of us makes this progression and that the sooner we knuckle down to understanding the new ways, the happier we will be. As I said, this is a working world and loafers do so here at their own peril. No one will force them to work, but neither will they grow or advance or develop or ever climb out of that embryonic stage until their own higher self tells them that the rest is up to them."

# IV

## Heavenly Computers

I felt deep sympathy for that poor fisherman with no one to admire his sensational catch, but Arthur Ford soon let me know that there were others with far greater problems in the spirit world.

"The types who have the hardest adjustment to make in coming over here," he wrote, "are those who either failed to believe in a life hereafter or were so totally unprepared that they will not try to adjust to the unexpected conditions. For instance, an avowed atheist finds himself waking up over here, after insisting all his life that there was nothing beyond the grave. At first he is astonished, then resentful, because he feels that this is hallucination and that those who try to help him adjust are fantasies of his imagination. Little by little he grudgingly accepts that he was wrong, however, and as dawn breaks through he is eager, even avid, to learn all about this sphere which for him had previously been nonexistent.

"Let us take another example of a person who was so sure that there was no God and no hereafter that he treated others badly while there and felt no moral obligation to lend a helping hand or to be a decent citizen. When he makes the transition he is angry and tempestuous, for he finds himself in a situation of his own making, surrounded by other greedy souls, who because they are in like situation, welcome him gleefully to the hell that they have created for themselves. He is shocked. These are not the type of people he wants to associate with. They are fiendish and ill-mannered, whereas he has been a stiff-necked, educated, and polished man, although he never gave thought to anyone but himself. He tries to break out of the fiendish group, but they surround him. He calls for help, but no one with better nature can enter the group to save him. He has dug his own grave, so to speak, and is allowed to lie in it for a while.

"He is utterly miserable, for he now begins to see the folly of his ways but does not know how to avert his fate. We let him remain there until his own remorse for sinful ways begins to penetrate his being and he acknowledges to himself that he wasted a lifetime, a rare privilege, by thinking only of himself. After he reaches full repentance he is then able to free himself of the unrepentant creatures around him, and for a long time thereafter he searches his own soul to review the past mistakes. This is sometimes a long, drawn-out process, because he will have to make his way alone. Only he is able to assess his wrongs and seek forgiveness, although there are many here willing to lend a hand whenever he himself reaches out to them for it."

Ford next turned his attention to persons who die violent deaths, writing, "Today we will discuss those who, unprepared to come over, find themselves suddenly here through no fault of their own, the victims of accidents, murder, or war. They are at first astonished to find that they are here and that those on your plane no longer recognize their presence, but if they were not antagonistic to the idea of a hereafter they will begin to adjust without too much delay. They sometimes sleep a little longer than those who, after a long illness, know that death is at hand, but when they have committed no great wrong, there are so many of us here willing to help them through the adjustment that they rapidly begin to understand and are sometimes more eager than the others to plunge zestfully into the new work which awaits them.

"Those who are full of resentment have a harder adjustment to make. This sometimes includes soldiers who bitterly resented being sent into battle and are nearly bursting with wrath to find themselves without the youthful bodies they had manfully enjoyed. This is not true of all soldiers and servicemen—let me make plain. I speak now only of the bitterly resentful ones who were not willing to give their lives for freedom of mankind and who felt that the war was wrong. They were in revolt there, and they continue here in a state of revolt unless kindly souls on this side are able to convince them that they are harming the soul's development; for it is useless to live in a constant state of emotional turmoil, filled with resentment at things which we are unable to resolve ourselves.

"Now we will discuss those who arrive here from a state of such inner turmoil that they have destroyed themselves. I speak of the unfortunate suicides. No person has the right to take the life within himself, any more than that of another person, since all are a part of the Godhead. These people, if suffering from temporary insanity, are soon able to overcome the aberrations which provoked the attack on self, and as their awakening forces grasp the problem and come to understand the conditions which led to temporary insanity, they will adjust almost as rapidly as those who came here through accidental death.

"Others are not so fortunate, for with their own reasoning power they deliberately set out to destroy their own body, thinking that they were destroying their soul as well. Since they could not succeed in the latter, their problem is far greater here than there, because no problem has been solved, but only postponed until the next earth life, whenever that may be. Thus, they are what we refer to as suffering souls. They live hourly with the shame of self-destruction and rage within themselves for having failed to settle the problem while in the flesh,

41

where it is much more easily faced than here. The means are not at hand here, you know, for solving problems of the flesh—therefore the long and often tortuous process of reviewing, reviewing, reviewing past mistakes in order to learn what this soul must assume as additional burdens when he again casts himself into a physical body.

"The murderers are, of course, in equal torment, having to face the horror of not being able to restore physical life to the one (the victim) who now is on this side, and suffering tortures for having robbed another of the opportunity to work out his karma in due process while in the physical body. There is no quick way to atone for such a sin against the very person of God. Thus, it is a miserable period until the person at last feels strong enough to reincarnate, with the avowed purpose of atoning in the physical world for what he did.

"Now we come to those who are sick and eager for death to relieve them of suffering. These are ordinarily the most easily adjustable souls, for they are joyously happy on this side. I was most certainly one of these, for although I wanted to do all possible while there to help prove the continued existence of the spirit, I was so plagued with pain from an ailing body that I eagerly looked forward to this release and have reveled in every minute since coming here. Those who make a normal crossover are delightful to watch, because their hearts brim over with love for fellow souls and nothing is too much trouble for them if another issues a call. Some work with babies newly arrived who are without mothers here. Others help the newly arrived who need mental or soul adjustment to the new plane, while still others assist with consolation for the bereaved who are left behind in your plane, sending them loving thoughts and easing their path for a time.

"Next we come to the type of individual who senses that he is in another place and time but who is unable to figure out why and where. He has not made preparation and has given no thought to the so-called hereafter. He will be bewildered at first and then so intrigued that he wants to ask questions of everyone he sees: 'Where is this?' 'Why don't people speak to me when I call their names?' 'Why is my wife going about her daily tasks without listening to what I have to say?' The whole concept of a hereafter, which is right here where he has always been, so baffles him that he is constantly running about seeking answers to questions that should have been settled within his own mind long ago, while he was still in the flesh.

"Unless he is willing to start a new period of development, he gradually becomes despondent. He wants to continue the old drive for success and moneymaking. After a time, some of the older souls here take him in hand and gradually gain his attention. They escort him about, talking with him about the exciting new prospects which await him as soon as he makes peace with the old ego that still wants to roam the physical earth. Sometimes a long period of time is required to make him see that this way has far more potential for development than to keep hanging around the earth people, and he is gradually weaned away from the ties that bind him too closely to the earth phase.

"Thereafter he begins to look about him here and adopt the methods used in this plane: quiet introspection, helpfulness to others, meditation, and thoughtful review of the life just passed. This will go on for as long as it is necessary for him to assess his past mistakes and reach the high resolve to do better the next time around. If he is still restless and eager to prove that he has learned his lessons well, he may seek the first possible opportunity to return to the flesh in another womb, and as his turn comes up he will have wide choice among those women who are able to offer him the opportunity he feels will best prepare him to meet the problems that he needs to overcome."

I asked for a broader explanation of the process by which a soul reincarnates into physical body, and he replied that the opportunity ordinarily comes only after the spirit has had "ample time to contemplate the sort of karmic debts it most needs to shed and to decide which qualities are most needed for further development."

"Once this selection has been made," he continued, "he needs to find a situation where he will most likely have the chance to meet the tests which will develop his personality and character so that he can repay karmic debts and advance. If patience is needed, he will seek a situation where his impetuosity will most often be put to the testing. If he needs to learn to love, he will have to select a situation where that quality is not in great abundance, so that he will test his mettle against those who have not themselves learned to give love. And so it goes. If he has earned the right to select his own parents, he will begin looking about for those souls whom he has perhaps known in previous lifetimes in the flesh, those with whom he has some karmic ties, either good or bad.

"Among those who have conceived and are expecting babies, he shops for the sex he wishes to be this time around and also for educational opportunities, if he is of high mental order. When the soul seeking reentry into physical body selects his preference, he must clear it with a sort of heavenly computer, as we laughingly term it here. This is a filing system so complex as to baffle and goggle a human mind, but here it seems totally logical, for there are always many souls simultaneously wishing to return to proper vehicles. If there is an overly heavy competition for one particular vehicle (or mother, as you term it) then the various qualifications are fitted into records here, which automatically select the proper soul to be assigned that particular mission.

"The idea of a computer in the physical world was carried there in the minds of men who had operated segments of this system here, and thus they tapped into the unlimited resources of this spirit plane, as Edison and others have done with their so-called inventions. 'Let there be light, and there was light'—remember? Edison's system provided that in physical form somewhat in the same manner as here, by harnessing natural elements which were always there for the use of mankind.

"The soul who wins the assignment then hovers near the parents for sometime to make sure that he is willing to proceed with a return to that physical body, and when the time is right and the physical blossoming occurs, he enters that newborn body, usually at the time of ejection but occasionally shortly before or after. If he hesitates too long the baby will not live."

I asked what happens with a stillborn baby, and he replied, "The body was not perfected, and thus a soul does not enter it. He will then have to start seeking again for a proper vehicle or wait his turn for these particular parents, if he was intent on living with them. The baby Kennedy was an example of one who, not finding it possible to rejoin his previous relatives when the body proved inadequate to sustain life, chose to wait until another opportunity—which never came in that case—so he is still on this side and now is often with his father and uncle."

Throughout the day I puzzled about this method of parent selection, and the next morning Arthur began his dissertation by writing, "Now let's speak of that heavenly computer which so intrigues you. When a soul wishes to reincarnate, he will file his qualifications (as he sees them) together with his reasons for choosing this particular vehicle as the means for reentry into the flesh. This free-flowing thought pattern feeds into a general pattern of thoughts of those who have also applied for similar types of parents or situations; and as the material is wafted into this thought pattern, the one most likely to succeed in that particular earthly environment automatically recognizes that he is the one selected. The others simultaneously are made aware that they should seek further for another vehicle better suited to their particular requirements in meeting old karmic debts.

"To those in the flesh this sounds nebulous and unconvincing, I realize, but here it is the most logical of procedures. Remember always that here we function through what most nearly corresponds to thought or ESP on the earthly plane. Since we need not communicate through sound or mechanical instruments, it is automatically made known through thought patterns."

I broke in to inquire about those who enter into deformed bodies, and Ford replied, "Surprisingly, there are almost as many candidates for those bodies of newborn babes as for the healthy, normal ones, for this is an important lesson which is learned here. The greater the obstacles in the physical body, the more opportunity for a soul to pay off karmic debts and achieve more rapid spiritual growth. The hurdles are stepping-stones if successfully surmounted, and the soul who in flesh body cheerfully meets and overcomes physical handicaps is growing much more rapidly than another who seems by earthly standards to have everything to live for. The reward is not in the physical form but in spiritual development, and the more hurdles that are overcome in a physical lifetime, the less often that soul will thereafter need to return to physical form to round off the rough spots in his character."

Next I asked about those who are mentally afflicted from birth or early childhood, and he responded, "These are such unhappy situations that we dislike even thinking about them. These are souls so desperate to pay off karmic debts that are holding them back that they are willing even to undergo that torture in order to advance spiritually. Sometimes they are deliberately assigned to such afflicted bodies as a means of atonement for abuses committed in previous lives. Other times, if they are truly repentant of serious sins, they will voluntarily select such a body, but in most instances it is an assignment by higher forces who compassionately select that body for a soul so troubled and tortured by past misdeeds that he is incapable of making his own choice. Medicine says that the injury to brain was due to malformation of the fetus or an injury at birth, and such, of course, is the case; but

46

the soul which enters that body at the time of birth or thereabout is aware of the damage and thus is paying penance for past misdeeds by assuming that afflicted form."

I wanted to know about severe injuries which occur later, in youth or early adulthood, and Arthur declared, "Sometimes it is totally unforeseen and is impossible to prevent because of circumstances beyond control of the soul inhabiting the physical body, but more often the soul itself has unconsciously felt a need for atonement and has voluntarily permitted an accident to occur, so that he may pay off old karmic debts."

How is sex determined upon by the returning soul? "Most often," Ford said, "the soul continues to be the sex that he has preferred in previous lifetimes, but sometimes he selects the opposite sex in order to learn certain qualities which are more easily understood by one sex than the other. Gentleness. A man who has been brutal will sometimes elect to become a woman in the next physical life in order to undergo gentling qualities and situations which require gentleness. Bravery. A cowardly little woman for hundreds of earth lives may then choose the body of a manchild in order to help overcome her physical fears.

"Now let's take the case of a woman with palsy who wonders why she should have to undergo such hardship when her present life seems to her nearly blameless. We find in the akashic records that in a lifetime in ancient Rome she was a cruel soldier who delighted in frightening others until they trembled with fear. He would turn wild beasts loose on tortured Christians to see them shake and tremble. Small wonder that in order to atone, this soul at last returned as a weak and trembling woman and by living a good life despite the palsy she can make tremendous spiritual advance.

"Consider a man who wants to be loved by everyone and goes about doing generous acts in order to gain the love of his fellow men. People tolerate his affliction because he seems so kindly disposed to others, even though they are repulsed by a giant welt on his face and neck. What a pity, they think, that this kindly man has such a heavy cross to bear. They are right, but the man himself was strong enough to elect that handicap, for in another life he struck a child so roughly across the face and neck that the bones were shattered and the youngster died. An eye for an eye, says the Good Book, and that is what all of us here know must be worked out before we are fit to join our maker or cocreator."

# Temple of Wisdom

The body of Arthur Ford was cremated, and in fulfillment of his instructions the ashes were scattered over the Atlantic Ocean near Miami. Less than a month later he began discussing a new facet of his continuing life, writing, "After I greeted old friends and had several chats with Fletcher, I began seeking for that which I knew to be awaiting, the temple of wisdom, which I had vaguely recalled from previous lives here and had sometimes half glimpsed during trance states.

"I had not long to seek, for without direction from anyone I came upon it, just where I remembered, beside a rippling stream in a half-hidden knoll beyond the first slope of a grassy hill. It was rustic yet so beautifully fitted into the landscape that it seemed to be a part of the lifestream. The teachers were awaiting and greeted me joyfully, happy to know that I had never quite lost the remembrance of its wonders and beauty of thought. The chairs were drawn up in a circle, and as I took my accustomed place the eldest of the masters exclaimed, 'Arthur, you have scarcely been away!' That made me feel good, for my seventy-odd years in the earth plane had seemed a goodly stretch to me, but here it was as the flicker of an eyelash. We took up our lessons where we left off nearly three-quarters of a century earlier, and it was as if time stood still.

"The master led off with a discussion of meditation, reminding me how important it is to continue that process here as well as in the physical body, for it is our enchanted link with the heart of God. This is why it is vital for mankind while in the flesh to keep at the daily meditation, for what he learns there is of the essence here and should never have a broken link. Even a newborn baby continues to meditate there and to feel unity with his creator.

"Incidentally, Ruth, the old souls who lead my particular discussion group here at the temple of wisdom did not have to consult for even a moment before giving approval for me to continue these morning sessions with you until our work together on this manuscript is completed, because they are as anxious as I am to have this word disseminated so that all may benefit from it. This will be of temporary duration, because when the task is finished I will go on to other duties which will help prepare me to join the masters as an instructor of similar-minded students who will be coming over here. It is part of my reward for remaining faithful to the trust while there and keeping up the daily meditation while spreading the word of it far and wide through my lectures and group discussions. Otherwise I would have been put back here as a lowly beginner again for who knows how long, since no record of time is kept on this side of the open door.

"Let me tell you a bit more about our temple of wisdom. It has existed in its present form since the beginning of time, and there were counterparts of it in ancient Thebes and Athens, having been established there by old souls who brought enough of the memory of this temple with them into physical body to try to create a duplicate of this sacred thought form. The counseling is purely mental here, but the spiritual so permeates every particle of the teaching that it is daily as if you had heard the most inspirational sermon of one's entire life-span there. The uplift is beyond description, filling one with the glory of God and the mystery of the universe.

"Picture, if you will, a grove of trees tucked into the side of a grassy slope, with sun filtering through and the leaves making a splotch of latticework in the glade. Here is our temple of wisdom—secluded, serene, housed in God's raiment of sun and shade. The birds are hushed as we commence our lessons of pure thought, but during the meditation period they pipe heavenly trills that seem to encompass the harmony of the entire universe. Ruth, it is a thrilling sound that vibrates to the depth of my soul and seems to link me with every living thing. How indescribable many of these wonders are, yet how similar are many of them to what each soul knew on the earth plane. The light here is pure and unceasing, since the sun does not control it. The mountains are eternally capped in halos of their own making. The trees are magically attuned, so that each seems to speak with a voice of its own. The songs of insects and birds are beautiful, and from out of the fastness of the universe come vibrations too harmonious to be conceived by the mind of a physical person.

"Let us take up another aspect of our temple of wisdom. Here those souls who are in a proper state of advancement congregate each according to his own needs. There is no single sermon or service, as in the earth plane when we met on Sunday for an hour or so to sing God's praises and pass the collection plate. Here each draws from it according to his needs, and the cup needs never to be replenished, for the wisdom is bottomless and pours forth in the amount for which the soul thirsts at the moment. No one is able to drink of the wisdom more rapidly than his own needs are attuned. Little by little, setting our own pace of development, we partake of this wisdom and sanctify our souls in the doing, for God is so near to us in this temple of wisdom as to be a flood tide of rapture to each of us."

As with the dictation from Lily a decade ago, I am

never able to remember what Arthur Ford has written through me, until at some later date I review large segments of it at once. But Arthur's memory is superb. The following morning he began, "Ruth, the temple of wisdom that I mentioned yesterday is not for everyone, but only for those who through long experience with soul development in the earth plane have acquired the facility to meditate and commune with the universal force. We who have earned this right are highly privileged on this side because, having refrained from wasting time in the earth phase, we are able to progress more rapidly here. I wish all those who eventually read these words would appreciate the importance of what I have just said. I want them to know the excitement and satisfaction that come on this side from continuing such studies into the spirit and soul of man. Then they are able to advance so rapidly that fewer returns to earthly form are necessary.

"Some of us underwent vilification on that side of the door, from know-it-alls who disputed our findings and poked fun at our endeavor to prove the immortality of the soul through communion between the quick and the dead. We withstood that ridicule, remaining true to our trust and to the inner knowledge that this was but one phase in a long progression. Those who scoff are to be pitied, for they are unwilling to stretch their minds sufficiently to absorb the idea that we are one continuing soul from the beginning to the end of time."

One morning I was feeling so miserable with a sore throat and chest cold that I did not drag myself to the typewriter until nearly two hours after the appointed time. Lily ordinarily opened the daily discussion, but on this particular morning it was Arthur Ford who wrote, "Ruth, this is Art. The others have gone, but I understand that you don't feel well and thus forgot about our date this morning. Used to happen to me too, when I was not feeling up to par. Lily's been here so long he forgets all the pulls of the flesh, but I hung around until you were ready.

"Today I want to tell you some things that may not have occurred to you. We here know each other through many many lives, some having been together at various stages in physical development, but all of us at one time or another crossing paths, here or there. As a consequence there's no such thing as a stranger here, which makes it easier for us to understand that we are all part of one another as well as of God. We souls are simply manifestations of the Creator, as are the trees and flowers and rills, but because He breathed the soul of Himself into each of us, He made us like unto Himself in that we have the power to reason and to know right from wrong.

"Right and wrong are not always the same to different groups of people, but within all of us is the innate knowledge that to harm another soul is to harm oneself and harm God. Basically, that is the primary wrong, for if we are helping others, even though we do it by the wrong means, we are at least striving toward the common goal of helping God. Now, if the wrong way falls afoul of the law, let's say in the United States, we have committed a sin against law but not necessarily against God. Such laws are often necessary to make it possible for large masses of people to live together in harmony, but the most basic sin is the deliberate injury of another person, physically or mentally, because our thoughts are deeds, either of commission or omission, and what we think against others is often as harmful as taking the food from his table."

The next morning Lily was there to introduce Arthur, who then wrote, "Hi, Ruth, glad you're feeling better. Now for the daily spiel. When I came over here, as previously stated, I thought that I knew exactly what to expect, having read a great deal about it and occasionally experienced the sensation of being here while in trance. But certain surprises were awaiting me. For instance, no one's whims are automatically granted without effort on his part. It is true that we are able to think ourselves into any locale to see almost anyone, but here are some exceptions:

"If no one wants to see you, you are not able to intrude on his solitude or other activities. It must be a two-way street. I might want to see Fletcher for long stretches at a time, but he has other projects besides that which he engaged in through me while I was in the flesh. Consequently I am not at liberty to impose myself on him except when he is also willing to engage in philosophical discussion with me or to show me the sights—for we have sights here, believe me!

"If I want to tell someone something at a given moment, he will not necessarily be available, for there are a multiplicity of projects going on here at all times and we are not at the instant summons of any other soul who might suddenly wish to see us. Am I making this clear? It protects the privacy, as in that phase you don't have to answer the ring of a telephone unless you feel like it.

"Some here are teaching new souls who come over, others are going to school to catch up with the philosophy and development courses which they failed to master on your side of the veil. Some are actively engaged in exploration of ideas or are trying to atone for past omissions by deep meditation and prayer. We are not so much closer to that so-called heaven than you are, you know. It is folly to think that because we swapped in our physical bodies for spiritual ones, we automatically have achieved oneness with God. Oneness is something to be earned after eons of effort to conform to God's laws and assist others on the upward path. The path will be lightened and shortened by every good deed which we do for others without seeking gratification of self in return.

"The will to give freely, without hope of reward, is the rung of the ladder to spiritual success. Let not thy left hand know what thy right hand does, remember? So stop hoping for gratification of self or earthly reward, but give in secret, telling no man and finding happiness in the doing rather than the telling. Why expect reward from

God if you've already had reward from man?—that is, praise and publicity over having helped someone there. We don't expect praise when we help ourselves, so why seek it in helping another, who is part of us and part of God?

"The temple of wisdom is not a place, of course, but a state of mind; for it is a consciousness of all the beauty of thought and awareness. We each no doubt see it in different lights, but to me it is the embodiment of beauty and truth. Within each of us is an awareness of truth. The temple of wisdom is a high form of that universal truth, and the privilege of studying there is one to be sought by all who wish to grow in understanding and development of self. Nothing is accomplished without inner effort, if it is to be of lasting value.

"This growth effort must be constant throughout every phase if we are to develop into a better people, a finer human race. Make no mistake about it, we have the power and ability to develop into what would be called a Super Race. But here's the catch: No man or group of men will be able to accomplish this. It is a total effort of the human race and that, dear Ruth, is why it is so important to help everyone in need of assistance over the rough places of life. Not a do-gooder's dream of utopia where no one is hungry and without shoes, but a human race revival. Once we were a part of a super race. We were close to this knowledge which I am telling you now and knew what to do with it before greed, avarice, hate, and other dire emotions gradually seized hold of the humans who incarnated into flesh."

The next morning I overslept, and after I had rushed to the typewriter, the writing began: "Ruth, this is Art. The others have gone, but I hung around in hopes that you would be able to make it." After a few jocular remarks, he wrote, "Now for some notes about the temple of wisdom. At the temple we are exposed to the greatest minds in the philosophic field: those who are here at present, and the benefit of those who have reincarnated into the flesh, for their imprint remains here, just as yours is here from other lifetimes in the spirit. We go to the temple for instruction in the so-called secrets of the universe. We learn the proper way to think as well as to meditate, for our thinking apparatus is a part of the soul, and that is why it is known there as the subconscious mind. It is always with us, whereas the so-called conscious mind is propelled solely by the mechanical apparatus of the physical body.

"The subconscious stores all of the knowledge we have absorbed since the beginning of creation. It is like unto the greatest filing cabinet ever known, except that while in the physical body it will not always be tapped in ordinary ways, since the store of knowledge is too great to be readily brought to the surface at any given time. Through dreams and meditation we tap into that great well of knowledge, and through proper hypnosis we also are able to surface some of the storehouse, though by no means all of it. Here it is available to us at all times, and if we develop certain faculties of the spirit we are able to expand the remembrance not only of the last life and the previous one here, but through the eons of time into other lives of ours as well.

"Here in the temple of wisdom Socrates has sat, and Kant and Jung, and many of those so highly respected in the earth phase. Here they are also towering figures of greater or lesser degree. Some great minds in the temple were never recognized as such on earth, but grew through the simplicity of their beliefs into great masters who serve well in the temple here. Many of them need never reincarnate, because they not only fulfilled their destiny on earth but have contributed so much on this side that their missions are complete. They are free to travel here through various stages of development to the very highest realms but are so devoted to service that they spend some of each so-called day here in the temple helping the rest of us along the way.

"Many souls who choose to learn and press ahead
56

after arriving here are not yet ready for the teachings in the temple of wisdom, for this is esoteric and they have not made sufficient progress in previous lifetimes to be ready for its teachings. For them there are many other schools of development where they learn not only rudiments of philosophy but begin to understand the purpose of our being. We not only were created in God's image but of the very stuff of God, so that in order to complete our circle and return to Him, we must absorb the philosophy of the universe and come to understand its laws, so that we never again will be out of harmony with this creation of our Father.

"At the lower schools the souls are taught how to absorb time. We become time itself, so that nothing proceeds without our cooperation, at least as far as each of us is concerned. Thus, if we fall by the wayside and loaf, we are time standing still, but if we are ambitious to grow and develop, the time within us moves ahead at a steady pace until that lesson is completed and we begin on another. Time is relative and different for each of us, for no two souls are in exactly the same stage of development. Wise old masters help us to move time ahead by opening the portals of the conscious and forging new paths for us to climb. This is an exciting world of growth and development; what a shabby thing it is for some souls to waste this God-given opportunity to feast our minds at the feet of such masters who have lived on various planes but because of their goodness return for a time each day to the plane where I am now to help us grow."

Ford stressed that all of us when we pass through the door called death almost immediately sense our "misalignment" with the harmony of the universe. "Those who sense this first are the ones most nearly in attunement," he continued, "for they realize the lack because they are so nearly in harmony that the offside is evident. Those whose alignment is way off center are so used to being out of tune that it takes a little longer for them to realize what is amiss, but all sooner or later become aware of this lack. Then they set about to improve the connection. These souls, whenever ready within themselves, begin seeking out a teacher who will set them straight, and the moment that the longing for a proper teacher strikes, the master is ready to appear. He is only waiting to be summoned, and just as the wish is father to the thought, so the master appears the moment that the thought becomes tangible.

"When the master appears, he takes the willing pupil to a house of learning where others of like thought are already gathered in study. They learn together in good fellowship, and although a few backslide even on this side, refusing to accept the precepts or the diligent labor necessary, most of them begin the steep upper climb in good spirit. There the rudiments of God's plan are expounded, the abiding faith in the workability of all things divinely inspired, and the essentiality of following God's laws without question. Here the more advanced souls do not even question the why of this or that, for it is so evident that if one defies the ordained plan he will fall in grace and become a lowly student again.

"The laws *are,* and that is enough for us. It is only the recent comers who are still used to having their own way in the earth body, or so they think, who try to challenge some of the precepts here, and this delays the progression of the soul. Had they spent some time while in the physical body studying the psychic patterns and trying to grasp God's precepts, they would advance more rapidly here, for learning discipline is one of the fastest of all methods for advancing spiritually—discipline to God's will, discipline even to the laws of the earth phase, which are devised to help men live peaceably together. Discipline is the lesson which should be instilled into every baby and constantly applied through all his earth life, for discipline is a cardinal principle here and even more important to those in the spiritual body than to those still wearing the flesh of earth souls."

# VI

## What Happens After Death

During the last few months of Arthur Ford's life, I knew that he was working spasmodically on another book, but I had no idea of the subject matter. Not until nearly four months after his passing did I learn from our mutual friend, the Reverend William V. Rauscher, that Arthur had already chosen his title. Strangely enough, it was to be called *What Happens After Death*. Within a few days after Ford's funeral, when he took over my typewriter for fifteen minutes each morning, he made plain that we were to collaborate on a book which would describe what life is like on the other side of the door called death. Arthur Ford is apparently a very determined soul who leaves no stone unturned.

Almost immediately he began describing the reactions of various types of souls, and on February 14 he wrote, "Today we'll talk about the kind of place one will find here if he has never given a thought to a hereafter—neither believer nor nonbeliever, just indifferent and too busy to give it a thought in the hurly-burly of his earth life. He finds himself in what appears to him to be the same place he left, only more so. By that I mean everything is more vividly colored here and the sky is without clouds, but other than that he thinks that he is still living and ready to go about his regular appointments. He rushes to the first one that he seems to recall, and although the room is full of people, he wonders why they all ignore him. No one will speak, and he racks his memory for some slight he had given them, but to no avail. Some of them are good friends, and he remembers having had no cross word with them.

"After a time he becomes so disconsolate that someone on this side of the veil who has known him well comes up to console him and set him straight. The newly arrived soul is scared stiff, thinking he's seeing an apparition of good ol' Charlie and when Charlie tries to tell him that they are now both in spirit, the newcomer thinks it's a bad joke in a dream. He goes home to find his wife, but locates her at a church, wearing black. He wonders who of their friends has died, never believing for a minute that it is he himself. The funeral begins, and he goes down front to see if it's any one he knows in the coffin. For the first time he sees himself in earthly form lying there and is appalled. This cannot be, he tells himself over and over. There is the family he loves, the friends and business acquaintances he knows best, and all are talking about poor ol' Joe, when he's right there trying frantically to attract their attention. Well, you will guess the rest. Little by little it dawns on him that he's absolutely trapped. They're going to bury him alive if he can't make them hear his voice, which is perfectly audible to him; and nothing that Charlie says convinces him that it isn't some horrible nightmare that will end in being buried alive in a tomb unless someone listens to him.

"These are tough cases for us over here, because having never held a philosophical thought in his life, good ol' Joe has had no more preparation for a so-called hereafter than a baby lamb shorn of his wool. It takes time, a lot of time, for us gradually to begin to convince Joe that he is immortal, that he's alive in spirit, but that the flesh is gone. His bewilderment and grief is often much greater than that of the widow he leaves behind, for she hopes someday to see him, whereas he will not accept that this is real."

The next morning Ford began, "Now let's take the case of someone who is expecting to find angels and harps floating around in a blue sky, with marble buildings and mansions, and a high throne where God sits all day and night looking benevolently at the happy souls. This is the view of the narrow-minded church people in small towns throughout America and elsewhere, but it just isn't true. If a soul who comes over here wants to will himself into marble palaces, he will be able to do so, because they do exist in the earth and we are able to go where we choose; but it's pretty hard to conjure up angels with wings and harps, because if they exist anywhere, we've never seen them where I am now. Rather, the souls themselves shine with varying degrees of light, because some are truly shining souls who reflect the aura of goodness and pure light, but we don't think of each other as floating around on wings. It's the thought that transports us, and since all solid objects on the earth's surface are merely thought forms, we move through them."

Another day he wrote, "Let me tell you about a station here in which some people rest for a very, very long time, until something at last awakens them to the potential of growth. The Catholics would call it purgatory, but the difference is that they think we all go there for a time, whereas this is not true. Catholics believe in praying for loved ones during this immediate crossover phase, and let me say that prayers do indeed help all of us here. We strongly feel the vibrations for good that those yearning, loving prayers provoke. But as to this immediate stage, this purgatory, it is a state of nebulism in which the soul hovers halfway between earth phase and this phase. It is not necessarily peopled with bad spirits but mostly with those who made no preparation or did not want to go on living and have immortality. So they sleep or move about in despondency and make no positive effort to advance, to learn, to recover from the shock of giving up the bodies which they had taken for granted and thought contained all the permanence there was."

Ford said that such souls may "lie in limbo" for a long time, morose and unhappy, until at last the idea comes through that they are holding themselves back, that no one can do anything for them until they themselves make the effort. "Then comes the true awakening, and at that moment there are many happy souls ready to help guide the newcomer over the barriers." In more normal cases, he continued, souls are first greeted by relatives, close friends or old classmates, so that they "at once feel the tensions created by a wornout body slipping away and youth returning; for we here are all in our prime of years, no matter at what age we crossed over. Even the babies quickly mature under skillful tutelage because, after all, we souls were all created at the beginning of time, and here there's no aging schoolmaster or heavy-handed parent to lay down the law to other souls—a welcome change for many on this side, believe me.

"After the initial greeting, the souls are introduced about and made acquainted with the laws which govern their transport and conversation with others, although little guidance along that score is needed, because they have already been conversing through osmosis, or thought-melding, or whatever we would call this when still in the body. Here it's more natural even than breathing is to those on earth, and very few souls with bodies have to be taught to breathe. Same here with communing with each other and transporting ourselves from here to there by the mere wish or desire to be there.

"As the soul begins to look about him and ask questions, he begins also to unfold his memories of past lives as well as the most recently completed life. He wonders why he failed so miserably to accomplish some parts of the mission that had been his goal when he took flesh the last time around. Now he remembers his aims at that time and begins to assess the life and see wherein he failed to accomplish certain portions of it. Why, he now wonders, did he fail to remember consciously while in the flesh these things which his subconscious so well knew.

"Now let's take the case of a child who came over here suddenly after being struck by a car in the street. That child is innocent of wrongdoing in that life, and no one is able to understand why such a blameless little tyke would have to die. But think! That little tot is just as old a soul as the parents who gave it physical life or the grandparents who loved it. It too has amassed its share of stains on the soul in previous lives and thus has debts to pay. Accidents seldom exist, for the planning on this side takes care of nearly everything except sheer, monumental evil which grows rapidly in a bad man's soul and overpowers the original plan he had pledged to carry out. A Hitler, let us say, who promised this time to be a painter and develop the artistic side of his soul but who, at seizure of power in Germany, let all the wickedness that had been developing in his soul through eons past take over to transform him into a human monster."

At another session Arthur took up the cause of those who, "having made the transition with full consciousness and knowing what to expect, realize that they are no longer in the body and cannot be seen by their loved ones there. Often they attend their funeral to pay a sweet farewell, and then, unless sorely needed by grieving ones, are able to step into the new role without taut strings to their earth life. They are the ones who make truly rapid progress here. They clothe themselves in thoughts and ideas and forge forth to begin new lessons and the exciting trail that hopefully will lead them onward and upward until they achieve oneness with our Maker. They attend schools at first, where the masters sometimes sit at the feet of the spirit souls and sometimes seem to float above them, but they are as real in substance as anything the students knew while in flesh.

"They teach the rudiments of knowledge, the Eastern philosophies as well as the newer ones like Christianity and Muhammadanism, and when this has been absorbed they go on to esoteric teachings of the type with which Christ was familiar when he walked the earth as the man

63

Jesus. They are not just laboring in the vineyard of the Lord but are actually setting their feet firmly on the path which leads to ultimate joy; for they are the chosen ones, as we might have termed them there, who awaken here with full realization of the pattern of previous lives and future incarnations. These are the rememberers, those who retained enough of their recollection of studies here that material man was not able to rob them of it on the fleshly level. We learn, for instance, that the best way to advance is to love, for an unkind or openly hostile thought about another soul retards the progress to such a degree that sometimes more than one future lifetime is required to erase the blot from the record. Speak no evil. Think no evil. There is no evil except that which we create, for I have seen no signs of a devil on this side of the veil. We are our own devils, with our thoughts and subsequent deeds."

I asked Arthur Ford to elaborate on the idea of the devil, and he responded, "Here we are taught the age-old wisdom once fully known to Homo sapiens but lost through the ages because of fleshly desires while in the physical state. We know that it is possible while in the flesh to overcome barriers of the physical body, if physical desires and hates and lusts are set aside. The temporal state is one of temptation. The challenge in overcoming these temptations is the most rapid way to advance to a higher state of being. The physical body is worn for such a brief period in the eternity of man that once this idea is grasped, the overcoming of physical temptation is not difficult. Why retard one's advancement, when for a fleeting moment in time there are temptations of the fleshly man? Keep this thought ever in mind, for it is paramount to overcoming the evil forces which surround man and would encourage him to renounce his Maker in the interest of passing pleasure.

"This evil of which we speak is not the devil incarnate, as some preachers would have us believe, but the forces and vibrations that emanate from those other souls who,

64

having passed that way, have left permanent imprint, permanent stain. Perhaps we are not accurate in saying 'permanent,' since goodness will eventually erase these imprints, provided that enough others sweeten the path to undo the disharmonious influences. There is a devil, but not as man conceives it. The devil is the force of evil which has been gathering in the earth since man first trod in physical form. It is the residue of that which is evil, and because man seems not to become more Christ-like, this evil gathers force as each passing generation leaves its own stamp of evildoing on the force that we think of as a devil.

"The devil was not a person ever but a force so powerful that it gathers strength with each new wrongdoing, just as good shines forth more brightly with each kind and thoughtful deed. In the beginning was the word and the word was good, which is, of course, God. The Father who conceived the earth phase for testing souls put no evil there, but the errant souls who eagerly inhabited bodies lusted, fought, and squabbled, hoping to enhance their own importance, thus establishing a force of evil which eventually came to form into a solid that they were wont to call Satan. Man, not God, created Satan, and he lives not as a wicked soul but as the personification of all evil, fed by every evil thought and activity. If Satan is to be destroyed, it will be done through man's awakening to the fact that even thoughts are deeds and that the devil shrinks in size each time we replace an ugly thought or action with a loving kindness. Thus we will approach the so-called millennium when good replaces evil in the hearts of those who inhabit earth, not only in the flesh but in the spirit, as we here are now doing."

I wanted to know whether animals achieve immortality, and Ford replied: "Time has no meaning here. We are ageless, having existed since the beginning, and we are without end. Thus we are *here,* and that is all there is to time. Having grasped this truth, we are ready to understand why it is that there is no such thing as waste. Nothing dies. Let me emphasize that strongly. Nothing dies. There is no such thing as death. All matter has existed from the beginning of creation, and nothing perishes but is transformed into various states, just as a caterpillar becomes a butterfly and then disintegrates in physical form as the spirit passes to yet another state of being. That is the key phrase: state of being, for 'being' is constant and never-ending. Thus the fly that we swat in physical form emerges into another state but does not lose its personality as a fly.

"The same with a dog that is run over by a car. The physical body returns to earth form, while the spirit exists as perpetually as any other spirit, to be reborn again and again. This is the immutable law. As we are in the beginning, so shall we ever be except as we improve our spiritual selves. Sometimes a faithful pet is so advanced in the physical state that its soul need not return to physical body, but that soul ever remains a canine, for what is a higher state than being a totally dedicated and loving spirit whose whole life is devoted to helping and protecting others? In the sight of God, that dog has reached perfection when he puts master before self at all times. What a valuable lesson for all of us to learn. We too achieve perfection when our thoughts are of others' welfare at all times, rather than our own Nervous Nelly apprehensions for self. We advance in whatever species, as we think of the welfare of others rather than our own."

Continuing, he wrote, "The dogs, cats, and other pets which we invite to share our homes and lives often show contrasting traits which are obnoxious or devoted. The souls in these lesser animals, plants, minerals, and birds are sparks of a different kind than those we know as man. They dissemble and fragmentize as an atom splits off into fragmentation, being incomplete souls who serve limited purposes and lack capacity to develop ever into souls of men. Yet the trees, the birds, the rocks, the animals, the beasts, the soil, and every living thing have personality and soul, even though totally different types of soul from those that we identify as man in the earth phase. These are living, breathing substances complete with sparks of God, and although none is as highly developed as the souls which assume human form in the earth plane, they nonetheless reflect the Maker of us all and respond to this love much as do those who become men and women in human form. They have their likes and dislikes, their whimsies and spurts of resentment. They go about their assigned roles and also try to become good and beautiful or ugly and bad, depending on their innate personality, which is a quality of the soul. That is why some of the growing plants respond to prayer and why others refuse to cooperate even though they are tended with loving care. Have you not known humans who respond in exactly the same way, some perverse and noncaring for others, some tender and eager to please?

"In the temple of wisdom we learn the power of prayer on every living thing, whether it be the healing of bodies or the striving for soul development. We learn that plants and animals and rocks and insects and everything which we are able to see and hear and feel and taste are influenced by prayer, for the Almighty God is supreme in His being and amiable to every honest plea for improvement of His creations. The wind in the trees, the whistle of birds, the whispering of insects, and the cry of man are equally heard by the Almighty One. Each has his own means of communication, and the God of us all has an ear always bent to these sighs and whispers and whistles and other forms of communication with Him and with each other. Do not think that this is a fairy tale. It is truth, Ruth, and until we learn to communicate with all other forms of life, whether in spirit or physical stage, we are not yet beginning to achieve oneness with God. Think of this at every available moment. Learn to listen to the voices of rocks and trees and stones and whispering insects and all forms of creation. Penetrate their secrets by sending this communication which links all of us together and makes every one of us a manifestation of God.

'Things' are no more things than we are. Each has its own form of life and being. Rocks are as much a part of the divine plan as are birds and bees and all of us. To each his own place in the divine scheme."

Sorely troubled, I asked whether we should then destroy harmful insects, and he wrote, "Fleas and worms and insects which stray out of the orbit for which they were intended will have to meet the threat of destruction by man, for there will have to be living space for each kind of created mass or form. The dinosaurs of ages past finally disappeared from the earth phase, since they had begun to overrun the preserves of man and all other beasts and birds. Let this also be a warning to man. If he becomes so numerous and destructive as to threaten all other forms of life, he too may face extinction. If these insects of which you speak become so numerous that they are threats to mankind and other beasts, they will have to go. We have our assigned places in the firmament, and if we exceed our missiong by disrupting harmony, we perish from the physical state, although nothing ever dies in the eternal sense."

How interesting was his comparison of man with dinosaurs and insects: Man, the litterbug of the universe. Twentieth-century man, who pollutes the lakes and streams, despoils the once-pure air, paves the once-rich soil with tens of thousands of acres of concrete, and depletes the forests. Are we thereby writing our own doom, as surely the mammoths vanished from this earth?

# VII

## Specific Cases

Ten weeks after Arthur Ford began taking over my type-writer for a brief period each morning, Mr. and Mrs. Wilfred A. Sechrist of Houston, Texas, came to visit us in Cuernavaca, Mexico. Elsie, an outstanding authority on the interpretation of dreams and other psychic phenomena, read with interest what Arthur had written and then suggested that I ask him to outline some specific cases of people who had crossed through the door called death. Ford cooperated with alacrity. The very next morning he began the writing by declaring:

"Today we have for you some news on the Kennedy brothers. Jack is at work on international problems and is trying to bring some kind of settlement between the Israelis and Arabs as his primary interest. Bobby is attempting to slow the pace of the impatient civil rightsers by cooling the situation. He says he thinks that he has had some influence on the more radical leaders of Black Panthers and such outlaw groups as those who are kidnapping diplomats and screaming for vengeance. Now to discuss their reactions when they came over here to this spirit state without the handsome physical bodies that they had to relinquish in youth.

"Jack knew no moment of unconsciousness. He was instantly alert here and aware of what was happening in the country he had led. He worked with Lyndon on easing the tensions and tried to help him get legislation through. Although he was not always successful while in the physical body, he wanted those measures to succeed, and thus he put his back to the load, so to speak. He feared that anarchy would result if he did not lend support to Lyndon, although he felt that LBJ's increasing involvement in the Vietnam War was a tremendous error. Even though he himself had increased our participation there, he had never entertained any intention of such large-scale involvement as his successor made. He wants now to bring peace to that warring world and wishes that he could make his influence felt as a mediator between Arabs and Jews, for he foresees dire days ahead in the Holy Land unless something is done to put some brotherly love into the hearts of those ancient enemies. His heart aches for those who are fighting and dying in Vietnam, but he foresees that this conflict will not go on too much longer. The hatreds in Palestine are of such ancient order that he fears a holocaust, without reasonableness now between Israel and her neighbors.

"Bobby left his heart in the civil rights movement, and he feels that this problem will never be solved unless someone of supreme stature wins the confidence of the hotheads and leads them into a more conciliatory temperament so that they are able to sit at a conference table to bring harmony while still insisting upon rights for their people. His arrival in the spirit form was such a shock to him that for a time he languished here, even though Jack was here to help him through the first days and weeks. The brothers have strong karmic ties and have been so close in many previous lifetimes that without the one the other seems less than whole. The close-knit family group was by prenatal choice, each wanting to share again his life with the others, for they were one family in early England in such pleasant surroundings that they pledged then never to be separated. Such pledges are not always easy to fulfill, but in the twentieth century by earth time they were able once again to find the proper vehicle so that all could again be one family in blood. Ethel [Kennedy] had been a part of that original family grouping, and when not able to come in this time to the same mother, there was never any question but that she and Bobby would find each other in the flesh again. They are as one soul, so close are they one to another since eons past. Jackie [Kennedy Onassis] was the outlander—but a queen whom they had known in England and were therefore able to pay homage to, while at the same time not accepting her quite as one of them."

A few days later, Ford returned to the subject of the Kennedys, after first writing this: "As we have indicated, the power of prayer is as important on this side as on your side of the veil that man calls death. When a loved one crosses through that veil, leaving behind his physical body, he is often bewildered and feels lost and forsaken. The adjustment is sometimes more difficult than anything he had encountered in that phase of life he has just completed, and because many of them had expected an entirely different kind of so-called heaven than we encounter here, they desperately need to have the assurance that God is aware of their predicament. Those prayers for their soul which are spoken in loving kindness by souls they knew in the earth plane comfort and nurture them and, make no mistake about it, God hears them all. Because this state where I now am is also one of study and growth, we are like you, struggling onward and upward in the hopes of one day being reunited with our Creator. Thus, prayers are vitally important, and the Catholics have the right idea in their prayers for the dead, a custom which should be adopted by all faiths and creeds and also by all those who still love those souls who have passed on to the next phase of eternal life. We here pray as diligently as ever we did in the physical state, and because this establishes attunement with our Creator, we feel its effects more immediately here than we did in the physical state. Sometimes a soul on this side is awakened only by intercessory prayer from those in the physical state.

"The Kennedy brothers are a striking example of the power of prayer. Such a tumultuous, spontaneous wave of prayers poured forth when the President was slain that he never really lost consciousness. Almost instantly he was attuned to what was going on, and because these prayers swept him onward and upward, he did not for even a little while have to encounter what the priests of his church would call purgatory: a state of souls wandering aimlessly and lost until something awakens them to the potential of their new state of being. Bobby also was helped by prayer, and also by the love of his brother who awaited him here, along with their older brother and others who had admired their vigorous fight for human rights. I was not here at that time, but I have been told of it by others, and that there was rejoicing here that these two souls had carried high the banner for human dignity, and that they were not required to suffer a long and painful span of years. Remember the old saying, 'Only the good die young'? Well, there is much good in nearly every soul, and not all die young, but when a soul is able to achieve his mission in a shorter time and still avoid the infirmities of old age, he is especially blessed. Some great souls live to a ripe old age and continue their usefulness, but sometimes at the zenith of a career, when the specific mission is accomplished, it is fortunate for that soul to be permitted to lay aside the body and continue his development on this side. Our temples of wisdom are so inspiring and so provocative to spiritual advancement that nothing learned while in the physical body compares with the excitement of these studies here."

The report on Jack and Bobby Kennedy led me to ask how President Eisenhower was faring on the other side. Ford promptly wrote, "He was a jolly good man who fulfilled his destiny by bringing peace to a sorely troubled world, but had he reached the Presidency at an earlier age, in less troubled times, he could have accomplished

72

much more for human welfare. When he crossed over here, there was tremendous rejoicing among the men whom he had led in battle, for they revered him as a father and respected the goodness of his heart. He is still leading many of them who had so resented their departure from flesh at an early and untimely age that they had built up antagonism against adults. Ike has reasoned with them and taught them that within the human heart beats a part of the Creator who understands all which we do not and that there are many perils far worse than death for an ideal."

General Eisenhower's monumental triumph over Nazism naturally led to a discussion of Adolf Hitler, and Arthur wrote, "Let us take the case of a Hitler, who seems to have wrought so much evil in one lifetime that he will never again be able to cleanse himself of such evil. He comes here after wrecking the lives and hopes and ideals of many other souls in the physical state, and he himself is an object of such scorn and horror that no one mourns his passing from the physical state. Here he thinks to resume his antics, his goosestep, his prattlings of power, but there is no one to listen or pay homage. This soul is so totally ignored that it is as if he were alone in a dark island without habitation. He prances, rants, shouts, to no avail. There is none here so low as to seek association with this monstrous soul. Shouting and strutting achieve nothing, so at last he falls into a deep pit of his own image-making, and into the black pit he falls, falls, falls until, like [Edgar] Cayce tells of Saturn, he is in outer darkness. There he is left to his own devices for many hundreds, perhaps thousands of years, depending on the severity of his crime against humanity. If he ever wakens again, his fate will not be a pleasant one, for until he has repaid at least some of his crimes against others by long and arduous study in this state of being, he will not be offered an opportunity again to return to earth life where progress would be faster. He has doomed himself to isolation for many eons, and the fate of Hitler will not be known to any of you living today, for his banishment—self-banishment, if you will—will undoubtedly take much longer than anyone now living in the flesh can perceive."

Next Ford made passing reference to Albert Einstein, writing, "A great scientist dies to the physical life and is greeted here with shouts of joy, for he has used his talents well in the advancement of pure science and the betterment of the human race. We are speaking now of one who has used his talents for good rather than destructive forces. This genius, as he is regarded in the physical world, is actually a gifted practitioner of esoteric knowledge who, with the assistance of other scientifically talented souls on this side, was able to achieve virtual miracles in advancement. The telephone, electricity, the steamship, and many others of like caliber, including the cotton gin, were joint efforts of talented souls on this side and the physical side, working together to bring about betterment of conditions in the physical plane. Einstein, who would nap for a few minutes at various times of the day, was actually tuning in here to the forces which renewed his objective and suggested the next step in his experiments. The moral for all is those nap times, when you as physical beings are able to commune with the spirit beings on this side to replenish energy, direction, and goals."

Elsie Sechrist had asked for examples of various types of souls: priests, scientists, orthodox believers, suicides, babies, children, savages, and the like. On March 26 Arthur wrote, "Today we take the case of a man of the cloth, a Billy Sunday type who preaches hellfire and brimstone and believes every bit of the Good Book literally. He comes across here, and after the first shock of discovering that God is not sitting on a throne surrounded by angels, he begins exhorting those of us here to repent before it is too late. He thinks that this is a very brief interlude until he adjusts, and that the rest of us are probably lost souls who lack the righteousness to advance into God's waiting arms. His sermons here actually do draw souls who hunger for the kind of heaven that their finite minds had conceived, and they think that this Billy Sunday type will lead them rapidly to the promised land. They throng to his sermons and shout 'amen,' while he tells them that within a very short time they will all advance into heaven with a retinue of angels playing harps. 'Amen,' they shout again, and are grateful that one of their own at last has arrived to open the gates of the temple. This preacher, whom we'll call Billy, at first rants and exhorts, demanding to know of the older souls around here how he finds the way to the throne of God, for he honestly believes that we are concealing it from him in some mysterious way. At last the old souls gather around and explain to Billy that he is preaching a false doctrine; that heaven is within each man, and so is his private hell; that he has arrived, and nothing is being hidden from him. It is up to him to begin work on his own spiritual advancement, and he is retarding the progress of others to mislead them with false hopes of a promised land. For this is the promised land, and we make of it what we will through our own endeavors. Wiser heads, so to speak, take Billy in hand, for he is a good but misguided soul. They suggest that he attend a temple of wisdom for a time to have his eyes opened to the one truth; that all of us are God, and that until all have realized this basic truth, none of us will advance beyond the basic state of man.

"When we grasp that each of us is as much a part of God as any other, then we are able to spread the good word that by helping these other parts of God we advance together to a higher plane of awareness, the veils drop from our eyes, and we are able to see exactly where and why we are here. Helping others is the watchword. Billy begins to grasp a glimmering of this universal law, and before long he is as zealously spreading this word to others as he was preaching hellfire and brimstone. Basically he is an excellent soul, but through mistaken principles he was spreading a false line. Now he spreads the truth with the same eloquence, and soon he begins to assess his previous earthly existence, seeing where he misled others by not opening his own eyes and listening to the persuasive arguments of those who were less orthodox than himself in his tight-minded beliefs. He is eager to undo the damage he has done, and through other ministers of like faith in physical bodies he implants seeds of wisdom, which if placed in fertile soil begin to sprout roots and spread truth among the hard-liners. Because he is basically a fine soul, he will advance more rapidly here than some who knew the truth while in the physical state but failed to work as hard as this soul had done to uplift and help others."

Another morning Ford wrote, "Today we will take the case of a baby newly born into the flesh who, after a brief struggle for life, withdraws back into this spirit state. The baby had wanted life, to be sure, and had at least helped to select its parents, but what happened to alter the circumstances? Sometimes the baby finds a body so weakened by malformation that it will not sustain life, but more often it is the spirit which withdraws. Let us take for example a baby born into a lovely home where he is greatly desired who lives only a few days or weeks or months before departing the body. That baby has almost certainly had something to do with the decision to withdraw. Perhaps at first there was a reluctance to enter the human body or the spirit became convinced that this was not the proper vehicle for working out the karma that obstructed its spiritual growth. At any rate, the physical baby's soul returns here from whence it so recently departed. Sometimes there is a short sleep, but ordinarily the soul has left the spirit world for such a brief period that little readjustment is necessary. Once again the soul takes stock of what has just occurred and assesses why it gave up the opportunity to become flesh again to solve karmic problems.

"The baby is not a baby, at least in the spirit world; for all souls were here from the beginning of time, and although some of them are more highly evolved and far wiser and more meaningful than others, because of experience here and in the earth states, none here is a baby. The one we take as an example today came back to us after a brief struggle as a baby in arms. The heart had been damaged in the physical body and therefore could not sustain life. The soul is disappointed at first when he returns here, for although babyhood is by no means an ideal existence, nevertheless he had chosen parents whom he loved and surroundings where he felt that he would be able to repay some karmic indebtedness. That this opportunity was denied him by physical limitations speaks itself of karmic patterns, for this soul realized that in a previous life he had ended the life of a new baby through neglect of its needs. Thus, although this was a life that he greatly wanted to complete, he had to make amends by withdrawing from that seemingly ideal situation. The so-called baby returns here and after a brief period of adjustment is ready to begin again in the temple of wisdom to learn how to resume the ascent toward the ideal of oneness with God. Because he has been gone from here only briefly, he needs little reinstruction, but if he had been a physical baby for two or three years, there would be souls here ready to help him adjust psychologically, to bring him out of the baby syndrome and into adulthood again."

Next, Arthur Ford cited the case of an older child, writing, "Let us take the case of an epileptic child who has seizures which grieve all those around him who love the little tyke. He seems to be normal in every way except that at times he has uncontrollable seizures. The child is not allowed to live normally because of fears that he will harm himself during attacks, and life becomes such a chore for him that at last his soul withdraws from the body without the normal span of years. When he awakens on this side he is at first fearful that among strangers these attacks will return, and he wails for his mother and father and grandmother, who have treated him with such loving kindness. He is afraid to open the eyes of his soul for fear strangers will seize him, and the mental agony is in every sense real.

"At last a famous doctor hears of his plight, and with consummate gentleness reassures the little boy that he will have the finest treatment. He works as gently on his mind as in the earth state he would have nurtured his body and little by little builds up such confidence in the child that he no longer is afraid. Then the doctor introduces other gentle souls who assure the little boy that he has nothing to fear from a body which has been abandoned. The child begins to search around him and discovers that no one is wearing the type of heavy bodies which were familiar to him. They are clothed in spiritual form more beautiful than earthly bodies, and all seem to give no thought to illness or pain. He revisits his home and finds that his parents, while sad, are no longer grieving for him because they are highly developed souls who think that he is now enwrapped in the love of God and will suffer no further pain.

"He blesses them with his love and from then on begins to mature rapidly under the guidance of masters here who teach him that he is as adult as anyone else. When he begins to assess his past life, he finds that he himself had volunteered for those seizures because in a previous lifetime he had been unfeeling toward the physical suffering of others and wanted to experience the difficulty in order to understand their problems. Soon he has matured into a highly evolved soul who, having paid off that karmic debt, is now better able to judge what it will be like in his next incarnation without that heavy load to bear. He wishes to learn humility, and because in that most recent life he had been favored with well-to-do, highly educated parents, he had been proud and somewhat demanding of their constant attention. Thus, he will choose in the next lifetime to be born to humble parents of loving demeanor but intense dedication to the aid of others. As the son of a missionary he will learn of the problems in many parts of the underdeveloped world and thus grow through humble beginnings into a well-rounded soul. Thus it is that the cycle helps us to develop, and by proper reactions in the spirit world between physical lives we grow in consciousness and develop gradually into fit companions for God."

Elsie had also asked about savages, and Arthur wrote, "Let us take the case of an aborigine who, having lived all his life in a pagan land without contact with so-called civilization, finds himself in the world of spirit. He is frequently less surprised at what he encounters than those of us who believed in Christianity and lived in cultured lands. He is familiar with superstition. In his land spirits were believed to be everywhere, and there was a God over all who directed the sun and moon and the firmament in regular pattern. He meets at first those who, like himself, had feared and loved spirits, depending on the natures which had been ascribed to them. They see their native land in detail and are more able to communicate with their loved ones still in physical state than are those who, through book learning and the admonitions of parents, have come to believe that no contact is possible. He revisits his old haunts, and when he sees that rain is needed, he allies himself with other spirits to try to alter currents of air so that rain will fall in their land. These aborigines are ones who have had far fewer physical lives than those who normally inhabit more advanced communities. Sometimes they have slept between lives for many thousands of years and are not yet fully awakened to the enormous advancement in the earth while they were sleeping. Thus, although their souls were born at the time of all others, they were backward physically and mentally, but not necessarily in spirit, because they were able to remember more definitely the days when man and God walked the earth together.

"Why do people not remember more clearly their previous lives and this spirit realm, which is the true existence? Because from babyhood they are admonished not to prattle about imaginary things. Very quickly they are enwrapped in the cocoon of so-called civilization, and although in primary schools they read of the so-called myths of Greek and Roman times, when fabulous beings walked the earth, they are not permitted to say that they too remember such happenings, however dimly. This forgetting is not only deliberate but sometimes necessary in order to block from the conscious mind recollections of previous lives in which dreadful things occurred that would cause them needless anguish in the physical plane where they now find themselves. They have volunteered to return and undo some of that harm which they inflicted on others, but to remember too vividly the cause of their present suffering could become an unbearable burden."

Arthur Ford next discussed the case of "a savage who had never been exposed to Christianity or any other organized form of worship except for the jungle cult." He wrote, "This lad died after having been bitten by a cobra and was about nine years old when he crossed over. He was as totally uncivilized as anyone who has never seen any form of cleanliness or civilization, because it was perhaps thousands of years since that lad's previous incarnation and he had done little or nothing in the spirit form to improve himself. He slept for hundreds of years and was so disinterested in other souls here that when he finally decided to try on the physical body again, he was like a fish out of water. He lived only to eat and sleep, and what work he managed to do was solely to avoid beatings and cursings. He lived in ignorance, and he died in the same manner, and thus progressed no single jot in that lifetime. For that reason there was no point in continuing his physical existence, and here, although kindly souls are trying to awaken him, he continues to sleep or thinks of nothing but himself and his pleasures, which are few, except that he likes to torture animals. Thus, the snake bite was in the way of karmic indebtedness for what he had done to those beings which are less evolved than human beings.

"This type of soul is highly depressing here, even more than in the earth life, for there seems little to jog them into awareness of responsibilities and soul growth. But even that boy was no worse than many who, living in civilized areas with plenty to eat and much work to accomplish, give themselves over to riotous destruction instead. They in their next incarnations may find themselves in circumstances similar to those of this boy who perhaps many eons ago had been equally destructive and thus was unwilling to return to physical state in order to repay his karmic debts. Growth, development, love, constructive action, and consideration for others are the keys to unlock the kingdom of heaven, and those who use force and anger to destroy, instead of love to rebuild, are earning dire consequences for themselves in this spirit life and in future incarnations."

# VIII

## Storyteller Extraordinary

Arthur Ford demonstrated his skill as a narrator when on March 30 he began a fascinating two-day discussion about "a man who thinks he is ready for sainthood and expects to be ushered to the throne of God by Saint Gabriel as soon as he crosses over here." This is the way he related the story:

"This man has told everyone that he has done no wrong and firmly believes it because he has never stolen, robbed, cheated, or misused his sexual drive. He has been a worker in the church and in charities and feels that this life is the only life in physical form before rejoining God in heaven. He has had a brief but incurable illness and has therefore had every opportunity to put his affairs carefully in order, leaving fair shares to his wife and children and to various charitable institutions. He passes over with a serene heart, and on this side awakens soon thereafter, with no protracted period of shock, because he was prepared for the experience of passing. He awakens here to see a beautiful landscape and at a distance notices several shining beings garbed in flowing white robes. He feels keen anticipation, sensing that they are coming to summon him to the judgment seat, which he thinks he has no reason to fear. The beings approach, but instead of stopping to greet him, they pass by on the other side of a stream that he had not yet noticed. Thinking that they have failed to see him, he tries to shout, but finds that he has no voice. He waves his arms, but they are not looking his way and soon have passed from view.

"In a few minutes some children come into view, and he wonders why they pay no attention to him. Surely he is as visible to them as they are to him. Again he calls out, but they pay no heed until he realizes that all he need do is impress his thought on them. Then they surround him with welcoming laughter. He asks where Saint Gabriel is, and they tell him that they have not yet met any angels. He asks how long they have been there, and none of them seems able to give a proper answer. A little girl holds out her hand and offers to lead him to the stream, where many fish are hurtling out of the water, but he says that he has no time for fishing. They offer to teach him a new game, but he tells them that his time is too important for childish pursuits. He will have to be on his way. He walks across a road and begins to search eagerly for some type of habitation. At last he spots a cobbler's hut and notices that an old man with a long beard is busily making shoes. The cobbler had deliberately chosen to appear as an old man rather than a young one for this occasion.

"The newcomer asks where the cobbler hopes to sell his shoes, since in the spirit world bodies provide their own raiment, and the old man replies that there is no point in selling anything, he is simply trying to perfect an idea he had for making such strong shoe material that children would not scuff or wear it out. The newcomer requests the way to find Saint Peter or Saint Gabriel, and the old man replies, 'The way lies within.' He thinks at first that the cobbler means a subterranean passageway, but before he can begin searching for an entrance, the old man adds, 'Tarry for a little while. Let the children teach you lessons in humility.' The newcomer looks about him but sees no one except the old man. The children have gone.

" 'Tell me, old man,' he then says, 'why is not someone here to show me the way to God?' The cobbler goes on with his work and waits so long to reply that the newcomer becomes restive. 'I have urgent business with the Father in heaven,' he continues. 'Where do I find him?'

"The cobbler lifts his glance for only a moment as he replies, 'Look within.' The man peers into the cobbler's hut but sees no soul other than themselves. 'Is this some kind of tasteless joke?' he asks with asperity. 'I am seeking the judgment seat.'

" 'I know,' the old man replies. 'That is why I bid you look within. Each of us must judge himself before we will be able to rejoin our Creator.' The newcomer looks astonished. 'But I have done no wrong,' he persists. 'My life has been blameless, and I am now ready to meet my God.' The cobbler sits silent for a few minutes before replying. 'But what of your pride, friend? What of your assurance that you are without sin?' The newcomer is nonplussed. 'But surely,' he cries, 'there is no sin in admitting the fact that I have lived a blameless life. I worked very hard at it and now expect to find my rewards in heaven.'

" 'You will find them here,' the cobbler responds. 'Here we find exactly what we have prepared for ourselves in the physical life. Let me tell you a story. In that life I was a priest, and when I was not teaching little ones, or telling my beads, or praying and leading services, I was trying to help the poor in ghettos. I too felt that my life had been one of complete and total dedication to God. I had never lain with a woman or taken a farthing that did not belong to me. I ate no meat on Fridays or holy days and kept all of God's commandments. A more blameless life I could scarcely envision. When my time came to lay aside my earthly body, I gloried in the thought that now I would meet the Holy Trinity face to face at the judgment seat. By earthly time I have now been waiting seventy years, and I realize that many more earth lives will be required of me before I am fit to meet God.'

" 'But why?' the newcomer cries in alarm. 'What have we done that defied God's wishes? I tithed, just as I'm sure that you and the other good people did. I thought constantly of purifying my soul. It is true that I ate meat on Fridays, but that was not against the teachings of my Episcopal church. Where did we err?'

"The old cobbler lays down his tools and takes the newcomer by the hand. 'Don't you see it yet, son?' he asks gently. 'We were too concerned with our own souls to stop and ease the anguish of those less fortunate ones. I taught the children their catechism, yes; but did I stop to worry with their mothers and fathers? Did I sacrifice my own bread that there might be more food for the hungry old beggar on the corner? Did you take time to listen to the personal problems of your employees down the line? What about your wife's frantic search for a calm and tranquil mind? Did you take her hand in yours and say, "Come, we will find it together," or were you always too busy with your own affairs to ease her troubled mind? She is happier now that you have gone than during the days when she felt that you expected her to look up to you as to a saint. Take a look at what your wife is doing now.'

"The cobbler fades from his sight, and the newcomer finds himself within the patio of his own house in California. Another man is sprawled in the sunning chair which had been his own, and his wife is carrying a tray of glasses. She looks healthy and relaxed. The man rises, kisses her, and exudes robust male vigor as he says, 'We will have a wonderful life together.' 'Yes, when the mourning period is passed,' he hears his wife say. 'Must we wait so long?' the man presses. His widow sighs and replies, 'I fear we must. People would talk if we married precipitously, but I can't imagine John really caring one way or the other. He was always so busy with his own salvation that I'm sure he would not care what hap-
85

pened here below.' 'Then you think he is in heaven?' the man asks. 'I am sure of it,' she sighs, 'but I do hope he isn't already trying to reform God. It's so dreadfully difficult to live with a saint, particularly a self-appointed one.' "

The writing ended there, and I thought this was all that we would ever know about the luckless man who had expected sainthood. But I underestimated Art, the storyteller. The next morning Lily wrote, "Here's Art to continue his narrative," and Ford immediately began, " 'Morning, Ruth. The man could not understand at first why his wife, whom he had protected and cherished, would speak in that manner about him. The old cobbler let him figure it out for himself, and as the wife protested that it had been nerve-shattering to cohabitate with a man who regarded himself as perfection, he began to see that he had tried too hard to inflict his ideas of righteousness on others, for they too were individual souls with a right to their own understanding. He saw that he had failed to enrich his wife's life with unselfish love but had tried also to make her his type of paragon, insisting on prominent good deeds that would draw praise from the community and enrich his standing with customers and clients.

"Now he began to look into his own soul and to see that he had been less concerned with serving God and his fellow man than with building himself up as a saintly person. Worse, he realized that by reaping the rewards for his good deeds publicly, while in physical state, he had not stored up in the spirit world any particular bonus. He grew to understand that anonymity of giving and helping was the way to reap blessings in what man calls heaven. This man suffered great anguish of spirit on realizing that the saintly life he had seemingly led had not really benefitted his soul as much as it had enriched his physical life. Without love for the giver, unselfish love, the community tasks which he had performed with great publicity had merely filled empty hours.

"The old cobbler was very understanding, for he as a

priest had given too much thought to his own soul's advancement, rather than unselfishly seeking to help those with whom he came in daily contact. The two men prayed together and rejoiced whenever prayers were said for them by those still in physical form, for they knew that such prayers are needed as much here as ever they were in the flesh. The two men who had lived so differently in the physical state now found close bonds, and together they decided to press their search for perfect understanding. They therefore left the cobbler's cottage where the priest had had much time to think over his previous life's errors and joined a group which was en route to the temple of wisdom. Now they are studying with us here and are beginning to comprehend that the mysteries of salvation are as plain as the noses that they once had on their faces: unselfish giving for others, putting the interests of others ahead of one's own, loving and doing for each other.

"This is the primary reason why each of us returns again and again to physical form, to see if we are able to put into execution that prime law of the universe which we learn while here. On this spirit side it seems so simple and easy. Here we blend in harmony with those of similar interests and vibrations, but when we return to the flesh we are thrown into contact with those who are not in harmony with us or we with them. That is when the testing begins and why sometimes we choose deliberately to join a family with dissimilar tastes than our own; for only by adjusting to them or working out a harmonious pattern of life that refrains from irritating and upsetting others do we advance spiritually in the kingdom of our Creator.

"When this man of whom we spoke eventually learned that lesson, he rejoiced that his wife had found a congenial soul with whom to spend the rest of her physical life; and because he had truly loved his family, in his own methodical way, he sent them harmonious thoughts and love to help smooth their path. Now he is advancing rapidly and is one of the most willing workers here with other souls who, like himself, expected to find God surrounded by angels in a room of gold, when they crossed to this single step in our climb toward life eternal."

A few days later Ford announced, "Today we will look into the heart and mind of a woman who believes that she is of saintly qualities and who expects to be transported directly to the arms of God. She fears nothing so much as having others in higher places of authority and is determined to impress Saint Peter with her virtuous ways so that no mistake will be made at the judgment throne. She awakens on this side and looks about her for the pearly gates through which she will enter after admission by Saint Peter. All she observes is a platform on which sprawls an old soul who has been on this plane since eons past. Mistaking him for Saint Peter, she approaches and says, 'Look here, sir. I am Mary Blunk and I wish to be taken to God.'

"The old soul looks pityingly at her and suggests that she rest awhile, but she will not hear of it. She had been sick in the physical body, and now that she has shed it she is full of anticipation for her seat beside the Father. She will brook no delay, so the old soul motions for her to pass along, and soon she arrives at a gate that is not nearly as magnificent as that which she was expecting. There is no lock and no gatekeeper, so she passes through and begins an ascent along a garden path. Flowers are blooming in profusion, but she pays them little heed, since she is bent on reaching the seat of God as quickly as possible. Along the way she encounters others who are either ascending or descending the path. Our heroine nods but rushes along, hoping to pass some of those who are toiling up the path ahead of her. Those who descend, she assumes, are rejected ones who are on their way to hell.

"Pushing past those ahead of her, she eventually reaches a high stage and assumes that on top of it she will find God awaiting her with open arms. Now she adjusts her hair and clothing. She feels them reassuringly, for the raiment here is as real to her as that which she washed on Mondays at home. She glimpses a handsome young man and, assuming him to be an angel, asks sweetly, 'Will you announce me, please, because I am in a hurry to bow my head at the knees of God.' The young man slowly surveys the scene and finally replies, 'But, madam, some of the newly arrived souls are still plodding up the hill which you have climbed.' She impatiently requests that he address God for her so that she will not have to wait in the long line that is approaching. The young man smiles and says, 'But, madam, how will you be saved until all those others who struggle upward are also rescued from the abyss below?' The woman replies that she has nothing to do with them, since they are all strangers to her.

"Finally another man approaches her, and she seems vaguely to recognize him as the old beggar down the street who was always holding out a tin cup when she hurried past his corner. 'What in the world are you doing here?' she demands of him. He replies that he has only recently left his battered physical body and is now in the next stage of development. The woman snorts that this seems an odd place for him to be hanging around, and she herself begins to mount steps that she has just noticed, which make an entrance to the pavilion where she assumes God is awaiting her. There at last she sees a man who seems to have a very spiritual face. Curtsying before him, she asks to be taken directly to God. The man replies, 'But, madam, all of us are God.' She looks wildly around and notices that he is including the old beggar in that sweep of his arms. This annoys her, for that beggar never seemed to wash and his hair had always been matted, although she observes now that he gives the impression of cleanliness. 'Stop playing jokes,' she says. 'Lead me to my Maker.'

" 'But, madam,' the beautiful young man says, 'He
89

created all of us, not just you, and He does not have time to welcome each and every one of you back to this temporary stage of development. The one over there whom you think of as a beggar will be a good instructor for you during this interim period until we are able to assist you and others to reach a higher state.' Such argument as the poor woman gives him! She will have no part of taking the beggar for an instructor, or anyone else for that matter. Her business is solely with God, and she demands to know where she will find Him. Others are now crowding around, and some are also asking for God. They all want to know where He is, and the woman is indignant that many of them have caught up with her, so that she will no longer be first in line.

"At last the young man turns to the throng of newly arrived souls and says sweetly, 'Hearken, God is everywhere. God is love, and as surely as each of you learns to love and assist each other, there will God be working among you. Now take up the mantle and see if it fits you any better than those who surround you.' 'But where is the judgment seat?' the woman demands impatiently. 'You are sitting on it, madam,' the beautiful young man replies. She looks wildly around, seeing no seat of any kind, and at last begins to perceive a glimmer of his meaning. She is to be the sole judge of herself. No one will tell her whether she has lived a pure and blameless life. She will have to work it out for herself, and as she begins to look within her own heart she discovers this terrible truth: In trying to live blamelessly, she has been thinking only of herself and her own spiritual growth. She was too busily concerned with her own goodness to think how to stop for a comforting word with those beneath her status. She had bethought herself to avoid contamination with those beneath her for fear that it would stain the white garments that she spiritually wore. Where was the love for others? Within herself lay all the answers. God would not have spoken more directly in His judgment than she was now able to do on her own.

She who knew her own heart best was now appraising her shortcomings. No one would judge her, for she was the sole judge of self, and when she tried to assess the qualities of the beggar beside her, she knew that not in ten thousand years could she see into his heart and know his errors of commission and omission, for he also was the sole judge of himself."

The next morning, Ford addressed himself to the case of a newly arrived woman who was grieving for the family she had left behind in physical state. He said that during her final illness she felt that she could no longer go on living, but now she feels so keenly the separation from husband and children that she refuses to adjust to the continuance of life in the spirit plane. But let Art tell the story:

"She watches constantly at the side of husband and children, trying to influence their every move and desperately seeking to attract their attention to her presence. Nothing that we say to her about beginning her own spiritual growth in this plane appeals to her. She wants only to continue living the physical life with the loved ones who, she feels, deeply need her guidance. She lives vicariously through their pleasures but yearns to protect the children from every temptation. 'Mother knows best' is her constant plea, even though to her they seem totally unconscious of her warnings. Souls on this side who are well equipped to work with those like her do their best to calm her fears and teach her that each soul on the earth plane must live according to his own light, without domination from others, either in our plane or the physical one. Her own progress slows to a halt. That which does not grow wastes away. Her soul shrivels and she becomes a pathetic person, without brightness or hope. She is apathetic, refusing to listen to the wise words of these souls here, even as she tries to force her will on those still living.

"At last she drops off into a deep and troubled sleep. This unconscious state may last weeks or months or years, but when she at last awakens she begins to see that her physical family is thriving without her, that they have made their adjustments to life, and that she is not as essential as she had believed. Now she is more amenable to suggestions from the souls here, many of whom have lived through similarly traumatic experiences themselves in years or ages past and are therefore best equipped to guide her out of her apathy. With wise counseling they induce her to begin her own spiritual awakening. She sees now that she was a destructive rather than constructive force in the physical state, too domineering over her children and too overpowering in her mother-love. She reviews these faults and determines to make amends. She vows that if given another chance to return to physical form, she will love with a light touch, freeing her loved ones from the intolerable burden of a too-consuming mother-love. She attends schools in which we are taught the difference between selfish and unselfish love.

"Now when she sees her children in their physical state, she sends them loving thoughts and a mother's blessings, without trying to dominate them. We on this side notice the change in those children. Before they were tied in knots, emotional and afraid of making a move for fear of displeasing mother. Now they subconsciously feel her radiating love. Decisions come easier to them, for they feel that mother is released and happy, whether they stop consciously to think of this or not. Seeing the improvement, the spirit mother is pleased with their growth and regretful that she had tried to dominate them. She gradually progresses until one day she will be born into flesh again, a wiser and more selfless person."

Perhaps because Arthur Ford was an ordained minister, he seems to relish reporting on preachers, as he invariably terms them. Shortly after Elsie Sechrist suggested that he describe specific cases, he told about "a preacher of the gospel who has influenced many people to become better Christians and in his sermons has preached of the Risen One and life hereafter.

"This preacher has had some doubts of his own from time to time about whether the Biblical descriptions of judgment day and bodies rising from the grave at the same time are properly interpreted, but he goes along with it because he is a sincerely seeking man who believes that the church is the best means of finding the path to the Father. He gives of himself unstintingly to help the sick in his parish and to encourage the flock to lead good lives. He seldom worries about his own future, because he feels that having lived a righteous life, he will be assigned to the chosen ones around the throne of God.

"Firm in his faith, he finally passes from the physical body and after a gentle sleep awakens into a lovely spot with a steeple and graveyard behind him. He feels at home, for this is what his teaching centered around: the church and the grave. He walks toward the building and finds it filled with well-dressed people ready for the service to begin. He hears organ music and walks down the aisle and into the pulpit area. Bowing his head, he leads the congregation in prayer. Music is heard again, and as he surveys the audience he sees few familiar faces. It is as if he were guest preacher in another parish, but when he eventually delivers his sermon he takes for his text, 'Know ye that ye are a sinner.' He wonders why he has selected that particular theme when he would seem to be judging these strangers, and he is embarrassed, but no one seems surprised. Finally he tells them that we are all to be judged alike on judgment day and then will be sent to heaven or hell.

"The audience smiles sympathetically, and he wonders about this odd reaction. He warns against the fiery torment of hell, and they begin to chuckle with kindly understanding. Now he is bewildered, until the souls in the audience arise with one accord and bid him welcome, saying that they have enjoyed his sermon and stand ready now to set him straight. This preacher is dumbfounded. Never has he had such reaction from an audience, and he begins to think that this is a dream from which he will awaken. But no. Now he is being led out of the church and into the cemetery, where he is shown his own stone on which is carved his name and dates of birth and death. 'You are one with us now, padre,' they say kindly, 'and here no one is judged except by himself. We're here to help you all we can and to listen to you whenever you feel the call to preach, but meanwhile begin your own evaluations of self and rest in peace.' "

Another of Elsie Sechrist's suggestions was that Ford discuss a case in which two people in love are unable to marry, and he replied, "Let's take as an example a woman who wants more than anything to marry a man who is already tied to a wife who is *non compos mentis*. They are in love with each other, but because of the laws of man he is unable to divorce the wife who is institutionalized and marry the faithful friend of his heart's choice. They live out their lives wanting each other but unable to be together. The ailing 'vegetable' outlives them both, and when they pass over here, let us say within a few months of each other, they immediately find themselves together in ecstasy. They are as one soul, for so long have they yearned for the comfort and joy of the other's presence. These two who lived ethically in the flesh will have one of the finest unions on this side imaginable to conceive, for although no such institution as marriage exists here, the melding of souls is infinitely more sublime. These two perhaps were twin souls in previous lives and had expected to find each other in that most recent incarnation, but something went awry. The man, having lost that inner-knowing of the woman he loved, met and married another before he found her in this past life. Thus the tragedy to them of life-long separation in the flesh. But make no mistake, each of them grew through that experience of sacrifice, and although it was not intended to be a separation, it became so when the man wed too young.

"They are together now, and nothing will separate them unless they at some time desire it, which is highly unlikely, for they have been together almost since the beginning of time. What is meant by a twin soul? It is nothing more than a melding together of two souls through deep affinity, where each feels strengthened by the proximity of the other. Some souls are more independent, just as a heart is used to functioning alone, whereas two fingers or toes are accustomed to having the other for balance or support. It is so with souls, some independent, others dependent, and who is to say which is the better way, for our bodies are projections of the thought of our Creator, and He made some of the parts of it independent and others dependent. Yet, taken as a whole, each is an interlocking part necessary to the perfection of the whole."

I asked whether souls in the spirit stage have sex identity, and Arthur replied, "No, we are both male and female—or, more aptly, we are neither, but simply a unique ego, each different from every other soul but possessing the completeness of a whole rather than a divided sex. Here, as we told you, there is no sex act since there are no sexes, but we are able to meld with those we love to such a degree that the union is far more perfect than in physical form."

I wanted to know the "why" of homosexuals, and he responded, "Those who return to physical body with sexes confused were not able to decide here whether they wished to return as man or woman and had such poorly defined urges one way or another that they retain some of this confusion. With those bodies where both sexual apparatuses are present, these are freakish thought patterns, and because of this rather unique situation, such bodies are sometimes occupied by souls who are unable to make up their minds which sex they wish to be."

# IX

## Reports on Famous People

As a newspaper reporter throughout most of my adult life, I have a highly developed curiosity about people. No friend with whom I exchange correspondence has been more obliging than Arthur Ford in tracking down answers to my many questions about notables, old friends, and those who have been active in the psychic field. He has kept me informed about the activities of my father and other relatives, but of more general interest are the fill-ins that he has provided about towering figures in the political, theatrical, and psychic fields. Most of these he has given in answer to my queries in behalf of this book, not because he fancies himself as a gossip columnist. I have assembled these names into categories, although they often "came through" at random, because whenever I typed a list of dignitaries for him, he would reply, "We'll look them up for you and give a report when we assemble the facts."

At the beginning of May he wrote, "Martin Luther King, Jr., is not here at present. He will not be around for a time, because he is working with newly crossed-over souls who meet death in battle, but we are able to see him now and then. Much of the time he actually spends at the battle sites in Vietnam and elsewhere. He bears no grudges and is too busy checking the welfare of his people and their rights in battle to be disturbed about the man who snuffed out the flame of his earthly life.

"Winston Churchill is often in conversation with Franklin Roosevelt. They are quite close on this side, and in fact have more in common with each other than with their own countrymen in many respects. Roosevelt seems fascinated by the British political situation, and Winnie is absorbed by the riots in America. Each takes an active interest in philanthropy and almost plays a game of seeing who will be able to persuade certain charitable men and institutions to do the most for his own pet projects. Mrs. Roosevelt is not around much as she is actively embroiled in the situation in South Africa and elsewhere, supporting the cause of the blacks and trying to get justice done in international bodies. Her interests are so far-reaching that seldom is she around more than a few moments at a time to check up on Franklin or some other relative or friend. Then she is off again on her peripatetic rounds to police the world and fight for justice for the downtrodden. A noble soul, but a rather exhausting one in some respects, as she lacks the serenity of some who would better leave some problems to God than to mankind."

What of Whitney Young, who so recently arrived? "He is already at the negotiation table. Hardly lost a second between death and awakening. A fine soul who earnestly wishes to win justice and fair play and who on this side sees that there are not just two sides but several to every problem, and he hopes to open the eyes of arbitrators and bargainers to this principle: not yes, or no, or maybe, but how do we do it together?"

Another day, after apparently checking akashic records, he wrote, "Now for George Washington Carver, the colored man—black, nowadays—who helped so much with the peanut. For a long time he was here where we are now, working with other scientists on both sides of the veil to perfect other products to lift the Southern economy: rayons, dacrons, textiles, and the like. But more recently he has returned to America as a black boy in Harlem. To protect his privacy we do not say who he is now, but he will be an interesting person to watch, for he was a white man before being Carver and because he once had abused slaves he volunteered to return as Carver to make amends to the race which had suffered at his hands. Already highly advanced as a white man, he took with him into the Carver lifetime the personality and scientific mind to help the lot of the black people.

"This time around, because he had accomplished so much as Carver, he was privileged to select almost any vehicle of any race, but he deliberately selected black Harlem because he felt that out of there must eventually come the salvation of the black race. He is now about thirteen years old by earth time and is showing great promise. His family is active in the political life of America, and that's all I can say right now."

I had asked about well-known political leaders of the past, and he wrote, "Now as to Abraham Lincoln, a shining soul with tender compassion for all. He too has returned to flesh after a rather long period here and now lives in New Orleans, where he is studying the Southern race problem in all its manifest facets. He is an adult, and he works with universities and foundations to find proper solutions.

"George Washington? He will not be around for some time, as he is resting after completing a recent life as a fighter in Vietnam. The shock of his death was such that he will sleep for some time. We prefer not to say more about his last identity, except that he led a platoon on a daring mission behind enemy lines and was captured.

"Charles de Gaulle is eagerly watching developments in Europe and the Mideast. He lost little time in taking the helm again here, as he was accustomed to do there, and now is like a firehorse in answering the call every time a shadow falls across his beloved La Belle France, as he calls her. He thinks more about the strategy of peace than of war and hopes to work with any peace mission that is empowered to settle the touchy Mideast situation."

My thoughts had naturally turned to the Soviet Union, and Arthur accommodated by writing, "Stalin is back in the flesh, but not in Russia. Went to another trouble spot and hopes to establish a dictatorial government, for he has learned little on this side. Still has the desire to spread the gospel of oneupmanship. He was not ready to return but did so when another soul stepped aside at the last minute, and Stalin assumed the newly born body of a child in Rhodesia. Sorry to report this, but you wanted to know.

"Karl Marx is still here and had no use for Stalin. They avoided each other with equal desire and, so far as I have learned, never even exchanged remarks with each other while both were on this side. Marx feels that he (Stalin) subverted his noble dream of the equality of man, and now Marx is trying to help the scholars put the whole movement of Marxism into proper perspective. He wants to be remembered as a molder of men's minds, but this is faulty scheming, for we should not seek to remember our highflown marks in physical life. It is what we did for people that counts. Whether Marx helped or hindered the forward thrust of mankind is not for me to say."

Thomas Jefferson? "Yes, living today in Virginia and still in his youth, not accomplishing too much. A problem with backsliding, when a soul had reached such a pinnacle of evolvement as Jefferson.

"The two queens about whom you asked have not been here for a long time but no doubt have reincarnated several times since their reigns in England and Scotland." He was referring to my queries about Elizabeth I and Mary Queen of Scots, and Ford apparently did not think it worthwhile to consult their so-called files in the akashic records.

I asked about Thomas E. Dewey, who had recently crossed over, and Ford wrote, "A fine man who is awake on this side and ready to go on with his studies. He's a doer, and a bright man to have around. No need to have any qualms about people like Dewey, who will put their shoulder to the wheel, so to speak. He is eager to learn and advance. Bob (Senator Robert A.) Taft is still here, and I've seen him and Dewey in earnest thought exchange several times lately. Neither is overjoyed about the way their country's affairs are moving at this time, but there's not too much that any of us spirits can do about it unless we are able to infuse some long-range thinking into the minds of the earthly hotheads. Taft is teaching over here, and Dewey will decide what to do when he has finished work at a financial seminar where he wants to help influence stock market investors so that the economy will revive more rapidly."

I had previously put in a request for reports on the progress of some motion picture stars, and Arthur now wrote, "Yes, Marilyn Monroe is slowly getting back some of her strength, so to speak, after a torpor which lasted some time because of the drugs and the suicide. She will be all right eventually. Has lots of friends and admirers on this side to help her, and she is repentant for taking a life that was housed in such exquisite form and rare beauty. She had been a very great lady in one of her previous incarnations, and this made it doubly hard for her to live the kind of gutter life into which she chose to be born this past time in order to learn humility and compassion. Well, she almost made it, and the next time around she will probably achieve her goal of saintly perfection, unless she submits again to lusts and passion.

"Clark Gable is as admired here as he was there. A manly soul with great potential for good, and he wants to help everyone, so we need not fear for his progress. He works with out-of-work actors to help them find employment to tide them over until the movies boom again, as that industry will do before long. All it needs is a good scrubbing of morals, and people will flock to the flickers again.

"Rudolph Valentino has been back in the flesh for
100

many years and is now happily married and living in Paris."

Suddenly I remembered that I had neglected to ask about my old friend Alben W. Barkley, the beloved "Veep." The moment that I mentioned his name, Ford was able to report without a moment's hesitation. "Happy as a jaybird," he wrote. "Young, frolicsome and as debonair here as there. Jane (Hadley Barkley) and his first wife are great pals, all of them laughing and studying together. The first wife was pleased that Alben found Jane, and they are a rollicking threesome. The Veep sometimes presides over the Senate and still wishes that he'd had a go at the Presidency. 'Never too old,' he chuckles." What a flood of memories that evoked! The disappointed "Veep" at the 1952 nominating convention in Chicago, when the labor leaders whom he had so faithfully supported turned thumbs-down on his Presidential candidacy by calling him "too old."

Because of my interest in the psychic field, I was particularly eager to know of the progress of those brave souls who had risked derision in earlier times to assert their belief in reincarnation and communication between the living and dead. At the beginning of April, Ford wrote:

"Today we will discuss Edgar Cayce, as you requested. He is here in a different plane and is hard at work on experiments for guiding others to use their natural intuitive forces. He has made some progress in breaking through the credibility gap in the psychic field and will not be available for direct communication. Some one of these days he will return to the physical, as he feels that this time he may complete his cycles of rebirth and reach a state near enough to perfection that he will no longer be required to endure physical hardships. When he came over here he was exceedingly tired and rested for a while, but now he is active in the A.R.E. [Association for Research and Enlightenment] movement and works with those who are able to admit him to their consciousness.

He is a fine man and a great soul who is revered on this as well as your side of the open door. His wife, Gertrude, of the past incarnation is also working with him, and since they are so closely aligned, they are as one person in the work that they are doing. I have not seen him, but this report comes from those who are aware of his commanding presence. Hugh Lynn (Cayce's elder son) is correct in believing that Cayce does not speak through mediums, but he will always be on tap for those who need vibrations to be raised so that the inner eye is opened."

I asked if Ford had seen Parmahansa Yogananda, the famous yogi under whom he studied for a time to develop his psychic powers, and he responded, "No, for that wonderful master is in a finer dimension and is said to be doing highly elevated work in more rarified atmosphere, so to speak. He is the embodiment of goodness and will be able to carry on greater works than most of those who have reached that elevation because of his highly developed psychic understanding and his long work in that field before coming here this past time. He is truly a master, in the best sense of that word."

My earliest introduction to the psychic literature of our times was Stewart Edward White's *The Unobstructed Universe,* in which he described the remarkable psychic communications between his recently deceased wife, Betty, and Joan (of Joan and Darby fame) who in 1920 anonymously co-authored *Our Unseen Guest.* The identity of Joan remained a secret until several years ago when Fletcher, speaking through Ford, who was in trance, identified Joan as Ruth Finley. In mid-February Ford wrote through my typewriter, "Betty White needed little time on this plane where I am now before she rapidly moved upward to the third, fourth, and fifth planes. She had done her work well in the earthly body and with her keen enthusiasm for esoteric knowledge was able to keep up the rapid pace on this side. Ruth Finley is also more advanced than this stage, and so are their husbands, who cooperated so well with their work on the physical plane that they too are able to advance."

Two months later, while describing the rapid progress which can be made on the other side by those who develop psychic attunement here, he abruptly wrote, "Such a soul was Betty White, who had often visited here while in the flesh and who knew what to expect on this side. She will not be on call for future mediums, because after the arrival of her husband on this plane they were able to advance together to a higher plane, where they are now working with scientists who need particularly adept minds to aid in their exploration of inner and outer space. They are adepts of a high order and while not perfected souls, nevertheless have an aura which is shining bright, for I have occasionally seen them as they go about their tasks in various planes."

Since Ford had by now seen Betty and Stewart Edward White, it was obvious that he too was progressing rapidly. As Lily reported to me about Ford, "He had a good head-start on so many who come over here because he had worked on it all his past physical life and was ready and eager for the next step."

Arthur also mentioned Joan (Ruth Finley) again, saying, "She will not be able to work with you now because of a problem of wave lengths and proper vibrations, but she is helpful when I ask her for any specific information that you need to know for this book. She is often in this stage, but only through preference, since her work requires her to be in contact with many of those still living in the fleshly form. She applauds your efforts to tell the truth in your books on the psychic and says she regrets not having had the courage to make her identity known while there and get on with the business of spreading the word to nonbelievers that God lives and that we are eternal."

I asked if Ford had seen Arthur Conan Doyle and Oliver Lodge since crossing over, and he replied, "They are still here, and we have had many fruitful conversations, as you would call it there. They are highly evolved and could have chosen to return to the physical world in situations of their own selection, but they are so repelled by the violence there that they feel better able to do their work here than there. They will eventually return, but not while your world is in turmoil and unthinking young people are rampaging up and down the land burning libraries and scientific buildings on college campuses. It is a sad state of affairs when the so-called young, who actually have spent as much time here as any of us, are so unenlightened as to try to extinguish the light of civilization. No world is perfect, but they were born into one which has reached a high level of learning and knowledge. They are the misfits, the incompetents, the hooligans who never adapted here and who, having felt their youth extinguished in an earlier age by war, are hell-bent, as the expression goes, to destroy that which would most benefit them if they pitched in, learned, studied, cooperated, and put their backs to the wheel."

I asked if there was someone else of towering stature in the psychic field about whom I should inquire, and he responded, "What of Emanuel Swedenborg? There was a towering light, a beacon for the universal knowledge of mankind. Never will that soul need to reincarnate in flesh again. What a monumental lift he gave to our work, and had only men opened their ears and closed their mouths, instead of vice versa, he could have rushed them ahead several centuries in thought and development. Seldom are there such great souls who give so freely of themselves, impervious to criticism from fellow man who considers them a kook."

Another day I asked Arthur if he had seen Houdini, the famed magician who conveyed a coded message for his wife through Ford while the latter was still living here, and he gave this interesting reply: "No, he's not in spirit state now. Already returned to flesh, and so has his wife. They're still too young for us to know what they will do with their lives this time around."

Then I remembered the mystery surrounding the disappearance of famed aviatrix Amelia Earhart a generation ago, and Ford responded, "She went down in the Pacific when her plane ran out of gas and was drowned. That is all there is to it. She and her copilot are still here and have smiled over the furor about their disappearance. They will not be flying in planes again for sometime, as they prefer it here, where they are doing some fascinating research together in the dynamics of combustion engines and radar superintelligence."

This discussion of aeronautics prompted a question about Virgil (Gus) Grissom, who with two other astronauts lost his life in a tragic explosion aboard a spacecraft during simulated flight on the ground. The next day Arthur duly reported, "And now the astronaut Virgil Grissom. A fine man who gave his life for an ideal: that of fortitude and achievement. Because he was cut off in his prime, at the pinnacle of fame, through no fault of his own, he will be able to reincarnate whenever the correct choice of vehicle appears, but whether he does so will depend on Gus. Right now he's actively working on a dynamic propellant without smog that could revolutionize air travel. Of course he keeps an eye on the space program, but his chief interest aside from a loving eye out for his family is this propulsion method of air or space travel which involves no carbon or fuels but is a method of projection with air currents at phenomenal speed, through dynamic thrust." Ford had already made clear that the usual means of conveying such new discoveries to physical man is through the implantation of ideas into his subconscious mind, preferably when sleeping or meditating.

Editor Ellis Amburn suggested questions about Beethoven, Ernest Hemingway, Napoleon, Bishop James A. Pike, and Pike's son who committed suicide. I passed this query along to Arthur Ford, who later reported as follows:

"First off, Beethoven has moved on to higher realms

105

and for a long time has been in the fourth stage, where he is undoubtedly able to produce music from the rolling vibrations of the universe with such awesome planetary sounds to harmonize into one cadence. He had been a musician in many lifetimes before becoming Ludwig van Beethoven, and with his deafness in that last life he repaid so much karma that he did not need to return to earth body. The choice is still his whether to return, but now he is in the higher reaches.

"Hemingway is a big bear of a soul, as he was a man. In some previous lives he had been a Berber and a Hun who fought for the sake of fighting and relished brutality. A keen mind even then, but a thirst for blood. Therefore Hemingway made great progress as Ernest Hemingway the writer, even though there was still some remaining thirst for brutality and excitement for the sake of exciting passions. But the unfortunate method by which his life ended has somewhat undone the tremendous advance that he had made. He will be working on this for some time yet. He had everything: fame, friends, wealth, talent. But he took his own life. Must never do it! Don't wish to talk more about this particular case. Sad."

After a slight pause Ford began again, writing, "Ruth, every phony medium since the start of spiritualism has been claiming to produce poor old Napoleon at her séances. Let's get it straight. He went back into another incarnation almost immediately, because he lusted for one more victorious battle. He found it in his next life, but as a weary foot soldier. Since then he has had two lives in Portugal and Brazil, also of short duration. But he is a doer who loves activity and does not want to spend long periods here in contemplation and review. His rebirths are not therefore to chosen parentage, because he fails to achieve that state between earth lives when he is accorded that right. But he's not a bad sort at all and swaggers his way along, rising or slipping from time to time, but no real evil in him."

Before relating Ford's response to the question about

Bishop Pike and his son, James A. Pike, Jr., it would be well to review Arthur's own association with the controversial bishop while both were in the flesh. Briefly, Pike's twenty-two-year-old son shot himself to death in a New York hotel room in February, 1966. About two weeks later, psychic phenomena began to occur in Bishop Pike's apartment at Cambridge University in England, where he was studying. One morning all clocks in his apartment stopped at 8:19, the time in Cambridge that young Pike had taken his life. Then safety pins began turning up in the apartment, bent open to that angle of clock hands. While two other people were working with Pike in his apartment, they simultaneously heard strange noises in a closet and on opening the door found the clothing in shambles. As they stared in astonishment, a shaving mirror belonging to Pike's deceased son floated gently from the top of a bureau to the floor.

On hearing about these and other strange happenings, Mervyn Stockwood, Bishop of Southwark and a student of psychic phenomena, put Pike in touch with Mrs. Edna Twigg, a well-known English medium, who brought the bishop trance messages which he considered evidential from Pike's son. More than a year later, in September, 1967, Bishop Pike and Arthur Ford were brought together on a television program moderated by Allen Spraggett, religious editor of the Toronto *Star*.

In the Toronto studio of the Canadian Broadcasting Corporation, Arthur Ford went into trance, while television cameras recorded the strange scene for a nationwide audience. Using Ford's vocal chords, Fletcher apparently produced Pike, Jr., who identified the drug he had been using as LSD and said that a "bad trip" had caused him to take the life that he actually had wanted very much to retain. A great deal of other evidential material, unknown both to Bishop Pike and Arthur Ford, also came through and can be read in more detail in Ford's book *Unknown but Known* and in Pike's own testimony called *The Other Side*. Bishop Pike subsequently lost his life while on a tour of the Holy Land with his wife, when he apparently became lost in the desert near the Dead Sea and several days later was found dead.

Thus, when I mentioned the Pikes to the discarnate Ford, he replied, "Bishop Pike and son, yes. Have seen them both. Pike was not ready to come over here. Had a lot of work he wished to finish, but had no choice in the matter. Could no longer survive in the parched heat of desert without water, and when he came over here he wanted at first to return to earth life, but not now. He has rejoined his son, who is doing better since his father is here and adjusting more rapidly. They were closer than they knew to each other in the past life and are now studying philosophy and other subjects, including metaphysics, to prepare for a return to physical body when the opportunity arises. They will, of course, review their past lives before becoming eligible for a choice in the matter of environment and parents. The boy will probably get a chance even before his father, for although he took his own life he was so doped that he had not intended to, and therefore it is viewed more as an accident than as a deed requiring great penance. He urges others to forgo the tragic kick of those mind-expanding drugs."

I had been reading books about Zelda and F. Scott Fitzgerald and, touched by the tragedy of their lives, I asked Arthur Ford about their progress. His reply was, "They are both here and pretty much on the same level, both squabbling a bit, but so closely tied together that no amount of quarreling separates them for long. Two peas in a pod, so to speak. She the more brilliant mind, but he the more brilliant perfectionist. They have been here long enough now that the rough edges are being smoothed, and they together are helping others with like problems of alcoholism to face the problem here. Not working through any writers there at this time. Too intent on easing the crossover for those like themselves who had more than a fair share of talent but lacked discipline. That is the necessity for brilliant young people who think they know it all. Neither of the Fitzgeralds had an ounce of it to spare, and here they are having to learn over and over the importance of discipline.

"In previous lives they were French nationals with a passion for painting, which they executed in similar fashion to the writing: bold, colorful blobs, but so little discipline that they frittered away their opportunity for immortality there. Now let's try to see them in perspective. He was immature and unable to focus his attention on the plot long enough to complete the material that danced in his head. She had the larger canvas but was so lacking in education and discipline that she was unable properly to combine the words with the thoughts. Much originality, but no perspective or philosophy to back up her words. He had the greater executive ability but was childish in his petulance and jealousy and envy of her splashes of word-color like paint on canvas. Unable to live with her or without her. Now they will have to learn patience, tolerance, compassion, and understanding before they are permitted to be born again unto parents of their choice."

Of Dorothy Parker, whose sparkling wit convulsed the Algonquin Round Table and titillated the nation while privately she attempted suicides, Arthur Ford reported: "Sad womanly soul who abused her body and her talent. Not true to the inner urges which tried to sense something greater than self in her last life. Before that she was a nun in Yugoslavia who lived such a circumspect life that she rebelled in last life. She had no use for religion, because of an overdose of it before in the strict monastic life. She wanted to be free of sham and the ties that bind, but she went to the other extreme. She will probably achieve balance the next time around because of her brilliant mind, but she threw shackles to the wind and thus regressed to the extent that she forgot the basic principle that we are all a part of God. Sad case! Resting now. Bemused. But will begin coming out of it when she stirs sufficiently to see where her errors led her astray.

"Her father was a stumbling block, but she deliberately chose a Jewish parent in order to be more liberal in belief, after the Catholic nunnery. Her mother was a good woman but unable to sustain life long enough to help the little child who had been a close friend in a previous life. Well, she will survive with serene spirit after she reviews those past lives and puts them side by side to see where the error crept in. Life without faith for Dorothy Parker was impossible, because she was so deeply imbued with it in her previous life and lives."

# X

# Proper Preparation

Arthur Ford is determined to get across the idea that those who have died are not floating around somewhere in space. They are here, just as much as we are, but in a different dimension. "It is all one universe," he wrote one day, "and we aren't anywhere but here where you are, although we do have a different *modus vivendi*. We don't sleep in your beds or sit in your chairs, but we do carry on our daily activities in the midst of you who are toting around that body of flesh. We intermingle and sometimes converse, but try not to interfere except sometimes to save a life or steer a person who is lost or unaware of his surroundings. Mostly we are moving through the same paths, except that without physical impediment we are not bothered by turning corners and going around rocks and buildings. They are not there for us, because we are a light and energy pattern, and so are they, and neither blocks the free-flowing of the other. We coexist with the physical beings and they with us, but the essential difference is that they are unaware of us, while we are totally conscious of them; and although we do not touch or smell or hear, we do strongly pick up the thoughts of physical beings, because these are thought patterns which are as plainly observed as deeds."

Ford said that those who train themselves to recall the

spirit life while in the flesh are better equipped to receive inspiration from the other side. "Let us take an example," he wrote, "a genius who on your side perceives universal laws and puts them into motion, as an Einstein, an Oppenheimer, or any of the great physicists. Because they were able to recall the universal laws, at least in subconscious state, they seem there to be geniuses, but actually they were highly advanced souls here with a bent for physics, and with the help of others here while they were in physical body, they effected seeming miracles. The same with writers who succeed far above run-of-the-mill —a Shakespeare, a Bacon, a Browning, a Victor Hugo, or any of the greats. They trailed with them into the physical state recollections of the laws learned here, and inasmuch as harmony is a law unto itself, never changing, they were able to compose exquisite music or the tempo of rhythm in writing, to enhance the literature and arts and music of the physical plane in accordance with the universal law of rhythm and harmony. Sonnets are an example of the universal rhythm imprisoned in fourteen lines of beat. Music which lifts one above his normal range of sound or above the mundane money-grubbing of physical existence is recalled by those advanced souls who brought memory of this phase with them. The cadence, the rhythm, the symphony of blended and harmonious sounds are reflected sounds from this side. Heard sounds are sweet, but those unheard are sweeter. So it is with our music here, for we are aware of rhythms and harmonious blending of notes which transcend anything heard there in the highest quality.

"Those who are able to attune themselves through meditation or dream to the real life that always exists and has been are the ones most likely to be termed geniuses in the physical plane. They are able to tap the source of universal wisdom and to put into play laws not yet discovered in the physical plane. Why, then, would not all earthly beings spend daily time in meditation and projection of nighttime dreams? Because they have not been sufficiently awakened to this source of tremendous knowledge and wisdom which is theirs for the tapping if they will but still their minds for an established period every day and listen to the forces within, which are capable of establishing contact with this other, this window of their soul, which opens onto this side of the veil."

For the past eleven years I have written about meditation, lectured about meditation, and urged meditation upon everyone with whom I speak about psychic matters. I have also practiced it, but never with the same diligence with which I urge it on others. I seem to lack the discipline which Arthur Ford constantly preaches. I know more "about" the subject than the subject itself. In my book *A Search for the Truth* I wrote that prayer and meditation are two sides of the same coin, for in prayer we speak to God and in meditation we listen to Him. Arthur Ford obviously feels that I need more instruction, for one day he wrote without prompting:

"Now let's speak of the value of meditation to prepare for this next phase of life. The preparation is important, for it brings understanding of the way and the light. When we go into meditation we are as near to God as we mere souls are likely to be for a long time yet. This is where we meet our God, within ourselves; and as we learn on this side, it is that withinness which makes it possible to assess our past errors and prepare either to advance to a higher state or return for another go-around in physical form. Thus, the more you learn about meditation while there, the more quickly you will be able to advance here. Remember in meditation to breathe deeply at first, expelling the poisonous or noxious fumes which our physical bodies often contain. Use the mantram, or the aum, and feel yourself melding with the universal whole. Become a part of it, whether the nature around you, or the essence of God. Become one with the living whole of creation, and as you sway to the pulsation of the universe, forget personal ego and all else except the oneness of the entire universe. After a time you should begin to feel yourself weightless and ethereal, and in some phases you will feel as if you are wandering as free as a spirit in an unknown realm. Keep trying. Hold the thought of perfect oneness, and soon you will be one with all creation. Go deeper, and from time to time let the spirit of God flood into the core of your being. Spend at least fifteen or twenty minutes each day in this stillness. Let God speak to you as He will.

"Now for prayer, which is totally different from meditation. Prayer is an active, not a passive attempt to touch the heart of God. Prepare yourself for this effort by putting from your thoughts all base and ulterior motives, so that you approach the Creator with clean hands. Think good, and God is there as you pray for His blessings on those in your thoughts. Seek also to be included in God's boundless whole. Ask for blessings as if you took it for granted that they would be bestowed, for that is the part which means faith. Seek to know His will for you. Feel His presence, and then be sure that whatever you ask is for the best possible purpose and not a selfish whim. Remember that the prayer is useless if it would harm another or put you above rivals and friends. Ask that God's will, not your own, be done, and then pray as if you expected to see the prayer granted in an instant. When you have learned these methods, you are ready for anything that may come afterward, for here we feel the divine presence with the same intensity that we feel His love, and except for those who on this side still refuse to pray or worship God, we are many times with Him in our developing consciousness. Some will go on to higher states of consciousness and will not return to earth life, and here's Lily to tell you something about that."

Lily then took over the typewriter, declaring, "As a soul tries to reach the heart of God, it will deliver his thoughts to such a degree that, without thinking of it, he will feel himself lifted, soaring free and filled with rapture. The sensation is so tremendous that this soul begins to

114

lose himself in the realm of pure spirit and will find that pleasures of fleshly life have no allure for him. Then he will want to advance here, rather than return to physical form, and the way is open for him to do so through prayer and meditation. I will not return to physical form because I have experienced the rapture of this union with higher forces and will not want to lose that pure ecstasy by wearing flesh. In the higher states of consciousness we are pure spirit, without thought of self. In that state we worship that which is the Godhead, and although we do not see God, we are at times totally attuned to His light.

"This stage of which I speak is not the ultimate, but another step along the path. We walk in the light of this presence, and for a while experience the pure radiance of that which is universal truth. We do not permanently stay in that light, for we are not ready for the perfection. Thus we return to other duties that we have agreed to perform for advancement of spirit, rather than returning to earth life. That is why I was still here when you rested your fingers on the typing keys after such a long absence until Ford came over here. I was still here because this was a task I voluntarily had assumed, and when you are disinterested, as you so often are, I will do other tasks, although here will I be when needed."

Lily has a habit of making me ashamed of myself, and this was no exception.

Ford never ceased to extol those who had prepared in this stage of being for continuing life on the other side. One day he wrote, "This morning we speak of a man recently deceased in the physical, who suddenly finds himself here in a total state of awareness. He has prepared through thoughtful reading, study groups, and meditation to do the will of God and to help others find the way. Thus, there is no moment lost when he steps forth here into his beta or astral body, and he is as assured here as there, for he has faith and understanding and tolerance for others. He greets friends and relatives and then goes

115

into quiet meditation while the vibrations of the universe fill him with quiet ecstasy. He begins at once to seek out those who need help, newly crossed-over souls who are lost or sleeping. This man loses not one second in lamenting for his lost body, for he knows that he will see his loved ones again in spirit when they come here and that he has left his affairs in the best way that he could devise. In other words, his books were in order before he stepped through the door, and thus his progression is constant and ever upward. Surprisingly, there are many like that on this side. Not all have known quite so precisely what to expect, but they were prepared to accept whatever God provided on this side and were especially pleased to find that activity continues here, with plenty of work to do. Not many would want to spend the rest of his days riding around on a cloud with a harp in his hands. Well, at least no one is tone deaf here, and all are able to project harmonious music if they are in tune with the universe.

"This man of whom I speak will progress so rapidly that before long he will be given opportunity to return to another body or to advance to a higher phase. It is unlikely that he will reincarnate immediately, since he has left no particular unfinished business and has been a decent, kindly man who deliberately harmed no one. Therefore, he will prepare for the next step through special work with the masters of the progression. They instruct in the beginning phases of altering vibration, so that one sheds the earthly pull as he gradually tunes into the higher notes of the next stage. Not until one has earned the right to do this will he be able to shift his vibrations sufficiently to ascend, so to speak, into the higher stratosphere. But remember that they too are here, except that they see us more clearly than we sometimes see them, for their vibrations often take them from our astral hearing and sight, just as we were taken from yours. Those who are more advanced are able to make themselves visible to us if they so choose for special purposes.

Lily, for instance, appears to me more as a brilliant white light than as an astral body of form and substance, yet his personality radiates as sharply as if he were in physical form. Lily tells me that I have several times previously gone into this next stage and then, after learning all that I felt necessary there, voluntarily returned to flesh form in order to put into effect that which I had learned. Such was the case before this last go-around as Arthur Ford, and that explains why I awakened seeing those rosters of names at camp, for in the higher stage I had learned to act as a receiving station for information happening anywhere in the universe. I vaguely remember that next stage but will look forward to visiting it again after we have wrapped up this project."

By contrast, Arthur next cited the case of a nonbeliever "who passes on and expects that to be the blessed end of everything." Instead, he said, "after a few days he begins to stir and show signs of life on this side. He gradually opens his eyes, so to speak, and beholds activity. He is astounded, for he remembers that he died and feels that this is a nightmare, like the last floppings about of a chicken whose head has been wrung. He struggles to end the delusion but instead finds some people around who call him by name and whom he remembers from previous association in the physical state. He squirms, protests, and finally demands an explanation. The friends of yore smile and say, 'Charlie, we tried to tell you before that we go on living, but you would not heed our words.' He squirms again and thrashes about a bit, because he does not like to be proved wrong, even in this new state of consciousness. His mind had been closed while in the physical state. He was always right, and he dismissed as a crank anyone who believed in continuing life. He tries to shut out the sight and sound but in a little while looks again, and now the scene is somewhat altered. Instead of lovely trees and flowers and friendly personages, he views a chasm, bleak and bottomless and threatening. He draws back in alarm.

"The chasm widens and he feels himself falling into it, deep deep down. He shrieks for help, but the friends are no longer about to reassure him. He falls and falls, or so it seems to him. Is this the path to hell, as the old-time preachers used to warn? Down, down he hurtles, his mind in torment. Where were those friendly ones who had gently mocked him for his disbelief while in the flesh? Why did they not help him now? But he had driven them away by his nonbelief, just as he repelled believers while in physical form. At last he begins to wish for their comforting presence again. He would like to ask them more about the eternity that they said awaited all souls. He longs for them as he descends into the abyss. The wish is no sooner expressed than they are there with him again on the grassy plain. He automatically thanks God under his breath, for the abyss is gone and he no longer is alone. The friends assure him that a wish is as solid as a deed, a thought the same as an act. By wishing for comforting friends and wishing to know more about eternal life, he had, through thought form, created the reality of their presence. He eagerly asks for instruction, and because he was basically a good man with good impulses, despite his closed mind, he is enrolled in the wisdom schools and soon becomes one who voluntarily assists other nonbelievers as they awaken to spirit form."

Another time Ford referred briefly to the nonbelievers, writing, "When such a soul finds himself on this side of the open door, he will not accept the fact, for he knows that there's no such place. When others try to rouse him from torpor here, he eyes them with hostility, believing them to be figments of his own imagination. He had expected neither punishment nor reward after physical death, for the places of heaven and hell simply did not exist, and he knew that his soul had perished with his body. For a long time this soul may lie in stupor, waiting for the so-called hallucination to pass away. He is vaguely conscious of activity around him, but to him it has no reality. Sometimes a soul wastes eons in this state, simply because the soul mind has not yet accepted the fact that it is alive; but more often the soul is able to shake off the grip of the stubborn physical mind and awaken to the reality that this is the real state and that he has now left the illusory or physical state, which was but a shadow of this real and thriving world of the spirit. Sometimes these honest doubters, who were fine but stubborn people with closed minds to the spiritual aspect of life, learn rapidly here when they have cast off their blinders. They are so eager to make up for lost time that they plunge whole-heartedly into the schools of learning and eagerly ply the masters with questions about immortality. But those with all-encompassing ego, whose minds were steel traps, will not recover so quickly and may lie in a semisleep state for a thousand or more years. There are a number of them here, and they are pathetic in the extreme."

Arthur told of numerous others who, having had no interest in immortality while in the flesh, reject the idea of a school for spirits, and therefore wander around various parts of the earth, engaging others in idle conversation. Such a person, or soul, is aimless and bored, making no effort to advance, Ford said, adding, "He may or may not return to a physical body with the intention of putting more effort into spiritual growth, but unless he does so, he will continue on the treadmill, coming into and leaving this life over and over and over without seeming purpose, because he has developed no inclination to open his mind and heart and soul to the spirit realm and the realities of eternal life."

To those who dislike the idea of a busy, working world beyond the grave, Ford has therefore presented an alternative. We can loaf if we like—at our own peril. I had asked Arthur what fate lies in store for murderers, suicides, torturers, and thieves, and on successive days he wrote:

"What of a murderer who deliberately kills another for his personal gain or satisfaction? This is not a pretty story. Full of hatred or vengeance, he expects to find nothing when he passes through the door called death, and for a long time that is usually what he finds—nothing. He is in a state like unto death for a goodly while, until at last something arouses him, and he wakens to find out that the hell he had every reason to expect is indeed awaiting him. It is not goblins and devils that he sees, but visions of his own face distorted by hatred, greed, malice, and other defeating emotions. He cringes from the sight, realizing that he sees himself thus, that he himself was possessed of a devil, and that except for his baser nature he would have been able unaided to cast him forth. He is appalled as he realizes that he not only wasted a lifetime of opportunity but that he set himself back many other lifetimes of forward growth. Now he begins to remember his resolves before entering that last lifetime. He had promised to overcome greed or hatred or temptation, but instead he met himself face to face in circumstances of his own choosing. Not for him is enrollment in the temple of wisdom or the higher school of learning.

"This soul will stay in torment for a long, long time, until he believes himself to be totally lost. When he eventually reaches this pit of despair, he may at last cry out to God to rescue him, and that wail of despair is heard by God. Other souls are sent to ease his suffering, and if his will is truly uplifted toward spiritual development, he will slowly slowly slowly begin to work himself upward until he has learned the penalties for taking another life which was given by God. When he is sufficiently strong to do so, he will accost the person whose life he took, and the reaction is such as to ring bells in paradise; for, as likely as not, the other soul has conquered self to such extent that he has already forgiven the suffering soul who cut short his span of physical life. This forgiveness uplifts the murderer to such an extent that he is gradually able to take his place in the society of other souls and finally to learn some of the lessons of salvation. Remember that a soul on this side, just as on your side, is never without help from God and the good souls whom God created in His own image. 'Ask and ye shall receive, seek and ye shall find, knock and it will be opened unto you.' That is the law of the universe. Ask, receive; knock, open the door of your mind and let the rays of universal love flow in."

I asked if Jack Kennedy has seen his murderer, Lee Harvey Oswald, in the spirit world, and Ford replied, "Oswald will not be awake for eons of time. He will suffer such repentance when he eventually awakens as to soften the hardest heart, for his was a beastly crime without purpose or logic, and the shock of his crime will be too great to bear for ages to come. Jack holds no grudge, although he feels thwarted that he was unable to finish the job he had so brilliantly begun." I also asked how Bobby Kennedy feels about Sirhan Sirhan, and the answer was, "He feels that Sirhan is worse off than Oswald, because he still lives with his bloodstained hands, whereas Oswald is unconscious in the sleep of shock."

In discussing suicides, Ford stresed that it is far easier to work out the causative problem while still in physical body than on the other side of the grave. "If a person takes his own life in a fit of despondency or frustration," he explained, "the solution will not easily be found here, for we have no right to extinguish that which God has lighted; and the privilege of a physical body in order to work off karma is not to be dismissed lightly. Others await their turn to try for spiritual advancement there, and if we angrily snuff out the life in physical wrappings bestowed upon us by our Creator, we will have to pay and pay for that in this phase, as well as in delayed opportunity to return to the body to work on karma which has now increased tenfold."

Ford voluntarily introduced the subject of a person who, having been abandoned as a baby by his physical parents, eventually meets them for the first time in the spirit world. "What is the reaction here?" he asked rhetorically. "As you think of it, you grasp the point: reunion. Laughter and tears in the spiritual sense. Why? Because on this side we are not willing to bear grudges against another, for the law is such that this is impossible if we are growing spiritually. Remorse? self-accusation? Better not, for it is a deterrent to spiritual growth. Put those emotions aside for the next reincarnation into flesh, when we meet self to undo our wrongs of the flesh, but it is impossible to nurture those sentiments in the spiritual plane without retrogressing spiritually.

"Let us consider another aspect. If a person was tortured by another in a prison camp, or on the battlefield, and they eventually meet on this side, what happens? If they are on different wavelengths, so to speak, without common interests to draw them together, they are unlikely even to meet here. But suppose that they do have sufficient interests in common that they are drawn into the same associative plane here. Does one forgive the other, or does the other reproach himself and beg for forgiveness? Not at all. That is a physical plane reaction, but here they simply accept that the one who did the torturing will sometime have to repay, by himself undergoing torture of the flesh. The other, the one who was tortured, feels that in some way he has by such torture repaid some past deed of his own and that the slate in that offense is now clean. We waste no time here in self-reproach or in wishes for revenge against other souls in the spirit plane. True, there are some utterly earthbound souls who plot revenge against some so-called enemy in the physical plane; and perhaps because he uttered an oath to "get even" with him while still wearing fleshly garments, he hangs around the person, vowing vengeance and seeking opportunities to balance the score against him. Some will think of this as haunting. It is childish and immature and wholly wrong, for here we are equipped with superior knowledge, so that the revengeful soul is turning his back on all of the feast of wisdom here to even the score with some poor devil in the earth plane. It is ridiculous, and such a soul retards his spiritual growth by tens of thousands of days or years, until he comes to realize that what is even worse than murder in the physical plane is continued seeking for revenge in the spirit plane, after we are fully equipped to know every right from every wrong."

I particularly like Ford's discussion of an individual slum dweller. "Let's talk," he began, "about a soul who wants to live a perfect life and has resolved to do so, but who is beset by so many temptations in a ghetto environment that he will not be able to resist all of them. He is poor, hungry, cold, and virtually unloved, so he steals to eat and steals to warm himself. When his time comes to leave the body behind, he is repentant of his sins but unable to repay the losses that he inflicted on others. He therefore arrives on this side full of remorse for what he considers a wasted life. But was it? He thought always of others, even as he stole from them to preserve his own body. He was not vicious but merely unable to resist temptation when he found the need of food or warmth. On this side he will first have to learn to forgive himself and then will do whatever he feels able to assist others in need who are still in the physical state. He helps them to find warmth and food without stealing by putting into the hearts of others the desire to help them. He wistfully yearns to prevent these other poverty-stricken ones from yielding to temptation. This man, by so doing and laboring long and arduously to assist others, will so elevate his soul that he will probably not need to return to alpha body to perfect himself, because his heart is right.

"Thus, a repentant sinner is more beloved than a righteous bigot on this side."

Arthur reiterated that there is no judgment in the next stage of life except by our own conscience, and he added, "This voice of inner conscience is a part of God, as we ourselves are a part of the Creator, but the judgment which is meted out comes from our own being after the bandages are lifted from our physical eyes. The veil is withdrawn, and we are able to see clearly where we erred and where we chose rightly and thus advanced perceptibly. There is a great joy as we realize that some of our most insignificant deeds, forgotten by ourselves, loom large in that advancement: the helping hand, the good deed done without personal gain, the sympathetic letter which helped a stricken person, the smile which we gave to strangers who were low in spirit. All these tiny, forgotten acts help us to advance more than one showy act of assisting financially, with great demonstration, for which we expected to store up credit in heaven. We equally find, with disappointment, that some of the things we were sure would help us advance here, in fact, retarded our progress. We hand out advice freely and think that we are helping. We overdo our profusive praise or flattery. We tell people proudly of what a great thing we did to help somebody. If we tell too much about our good deeds there, we receive ample reward in the physical state, so it stores up nothing to our account here. Let not the left hand know what the right hand does. Forget it. When we are in spirit we take with us none of the good deeds for which we have earned reward in the physical state. But how richly we reap reward for that which we did solely because another needed us, expecting no thanks or reward. Bear no resentments, then, toward those who seem unappreciative there. Help when you are able and then forget it. Go through life as an instrument of the Creator, asking nothing for yourself except that for which you work in order to live comfortably. Forget about publicized alms and make yourself a well which will never run dry, because bubbling up from that well is love which, freely given, continually pumps up more love to overflowing."

# XI

# Conquer Those Bad Habits

If there is any subject that I dislike to think about, it is bad habits, because I seem to have so many of them. Readers of *A Search for the Truth* will recall that Lily succeeded in persuading me to give up cigarette smoking; but two years later, having been unable to shed the unwelcome ten pounds which nonsmoking produced, I returned to the filthy habit. I still like a cocktail or two before dinner, and I am conscious of a caustic tongue which I sometimes fail to control.

My old friend Arthur Ford was a gentle man, but he collected his own share of bad habits. Through no fault of his own, he was for a time addicted to drugs, and in order to overcome that problem he became an alcoholic to such degree that even in his last years, he occasionally fell off the wagon, with near-disastrous results. He smoked an occasional cigarette, although he was by no means an addict in this respect. Consequently, I expected far more understanding from the spirit Ford than from my stern guide, Lily, but Arthur soon took me to task for these frailties of the flesh.

The first mention of cigarettes came on March 1, when Lily wrote, "Ruth, it would be so much easier for us to project, and you to receive, if you were not filled with smoke, for it impedes the progress and is like a smokescreen in the world that you are in there. We find it difficult to permeate the fog, so why not give up smoking now, and let's get on with the work of this book." After a few more pertinent remarks, he wrote, "All right. Here's Art, who did not want to be the one to give you reproofs."

Ten days later, after discussing certain laws of the universe, Ford wrote, "We learn now why the problem so often arises here of wanting to return again and again to physical state, without spending enough time to assess all errors of the previous round and determine exactly how we expect to meet future temptations as they arise. Why would a soul want to rush back to earth form before he is ready? Here we face the failing in so-called human nature: the zest for pleasures of the flesh, desire for too much alcohol, sex, body-building, and the like. Some are so overly fond of the bodies they left behind that they are scarcely able to wait for an opportunity to form another body and set to work indulging it. These souls are the truly earthbound, who will not be able to advance spiritually until they learn to give less thought to appetites of the flesh. Any habit-forming pleasure, and they are endless, traps one into the cycle of rebirth over and over, until the appetites are finally put aside while still in the flesh—lust for money, lust for power, lust for sex, and habits such as an unnatural craving for alcohol, drugs, tobacco, or any of the indulgences which we feel unable to break loose from. This is a lesson for souls who would like to break the cycle of rebirth. See what I mean?

"Drunks on this side hover around the earth souls who drink too much, lusting after the pleasures of alcoholism and unable to break the bond of habit which binds them to physical body. The same with heavy smokers or drug users, there or here, or the sex maniacs who take advantage of others to appease the bodily craving for intercourse. This is a very important lesson which we learn on this side. To escape the perpetual cycle of rebirth into physical form, we must erase the ties, the shackles which bind us to satiation of the physical body. So try to lick

126

the bad habits while there. It is easier far than to come unloose from them on this side. Those who neither drink nor smoke nor use drugs nor lust after sex will be free of those shackles on this side.

"But one must also remember that misers who hoard wealth instead of sharing it will have the same trouble over here. Those who are zealots in any line, whether politics or religion or whatever, and who lack tolerance for the beliefs of others will still be trying to run everything on this side, telling others how to think and act, unless they iron out those flaws of personality in the body form. In other words, we are no better and no worse than those who still inhabit physical forms. We take with us the same flaws of character, the same cravings and shackles as we had while in the stage where you are now. And until those flaws are mended, we do not advance spiritually to any marked degree. That is why we return over and over to the earth form, hoping to erase those flaws and overcome the bonds which hold us back.

"It is easier while in physical form to break those shackles than it is to undo them here, where no temptations are put in our way. Thus, there is no reward for behaving correctly here in spirit, because there is nothing to tempt us otherwise. The hard school is in the physical one, and there it is that we must meet and overcome the temptations."

A week or so later, Arthur wrote, "Today we take the case of a person who has everything to live for but begins taking drugs and so loses interest in those about him that he eventually takes his life. This life which was given to him by God was not, of course, his to take, but his mind was so befuddled that he scarcely realized that he was quenching the spark. As he awakens here, still in a drugged state, and begins to search for another shot of morphine or looks about for a pusher from whom to buy whichever drug was his favorite, he sees many souls milling about that level, but none seems to know where he will be able to buy dope. Some look at him pityingly, but others are as indifferent to his needs as many on the physical plane would have been, for this is a lowly crossover point where only earthbound souls are fore-gathered. His search impels him to rush frantically about, so doped in his mind that he is not even aware that he no longer is in fleshly garb. His spirit craves the drugs as overwhelmingly as his physical body would have done. He flings himself to the ground and claws the turf with his fingernails, for in thought form these are as real to him as in physical form. He whimpers, begs, and weeps. He will have to have drugs, or his sanity will leave him, he firmly believes. Then he begins to rail at God, screaming that there is no mercy. In the spirit state he is as totally drugged as in the physical—a complete addict who cares nothing for self or others, but only for release from suffering by means of drugs.

"At last he falls into a torpor, and this may last for months or eons, for the destruction of mind and weakening of physical forces in the earth state have so diseased his soul mind that he is unfit for spiritual growth for a long, long time. In some instances he may sleep for hundreds of years, totally unaware of his surroundings, and by the time he eventually begins to stir no one is left on earth in the physical form whom he would recognize. The newly arrived souls around him have no awareness of him or his identity. He is indeed a lost soul, for he knows no one and has no inkling of his state; those whom he once loved or knew have long since advanced to higher levels or have once again incarnated into physical body under new names and identities. He seems lost to all help, and his lethargy may continue for a long time after he awakens from his drugged sleep, for there is no one around who arouses a spark of interest from him. His apathy repels any who would advance to help him. He gives forth no light or spark and is withdrawn within himself.

"This condition may again last dozens or hundreds of years, until at last he cries out to God to help him. God hears, as He would have heard the faintest murmur hundreds of years before if the plea for surcease from suffering had been uttered. But the effort must come from within each of us. God waits until our own need brings us to His feet. Immediately old souls gather around him, and he is lifted up and taken to a sanitarium where others of like condition are already undergoing treatment. Some are being soothed from withdrawal symptoms, because they immediately called on God for assistance. Some, like this man, have slept for eons and no longer have withdrawal pangs but need assistance in taking up their life again. They need to be reawakened to the spiritual spark within and to be nurtured and taught once again that all of us are God. At last the man begins to respond to treatment and to grow again in grace and strength, understanding at last why he was unable to reach out to God while he was so drugged that his higher self slept. He vows never again to be tempted by anything which affects his mental range, and before he again volunteers for earthly rebirth he strengthens this vow by offering to work among those who are disoriented and diseased in mind or spirit."

On April 5 I asked Ford whether he had learned what karmic debt led to his automobile accident, which in turn led to the morphine and alcohol addiction. He replied forthrightly, "Only too well. From a previous record I see that I was a drunkard who had no thought for anyone but myself and my bottle. I died in the gutter, so to speak, in that life in Pennsylvania during the Colonial period. And although I was good-hearted, liquor proved to be my downfall, for its hold on me was stronger than that of a family whom I sacrificed to its tug. When I entered the physical world again as Arthur Ford, it was with a firm resolve to atone and live a spiritual life. As you know from my book (*Nothing So Strange*) and our talks together, this was the pattern of my youth, and I might have lived out my life as a stuffy preacher in the hills of West Virginia or Kentucky, except that my eyes were opened through dreams to an earlier life as a seer in ancient Egypt. For a time these two determinations lived happily together, until through physical and mental exhaustion I opened that other window into the life as a wastrel drunk. The opportunity to overcome that karma was presented by the accident which, as far as I know, had not been planned, although who will ever be sure, since two women died in that accident.

"Anyway, the temptation was handed to me, and because of that previous life as a wastrel my spirit subconsciously embraced the old friend liquor. It was no friend, believe me! Because of that wasted life in Pennsylvania, I had built up such tolerance and capacity for liquor that it took an awful lot of it to get me tight in this past life. Would that it had not been so, for a little of it now and then might not have hurt me; but the karmic pattern of the Pennsylvania life was too much for my high resolve, and it's a wonder that it did not utterly destroy my most recent life as well. Thank God for friends with understanding natures who kept an eye out for my welfare and helped to get me back on the right track whenever I slipped. Now, through tenacious fighting against the old demon, I think the problem for me is licked. I had not willfully sought liquor, and except for that fool doctor I probably would never have tasted it in my life as Arthur Ford."

A few days after that sad confessional, Arthur wrote, "We will want you to put into the book a great deal of the inspirational things that made *A Search for the Truth* so valuable to many seeking and distraught people. Therefore, today let's talk a bit about those high-minded subjects at which Lily is so adept. Here's Lily."

Lily then took over the typewriter with this message: "Ruth, unless a soul sufficiently strives for perfection while in physical form, he is actually losing ground, because on this side the laws are such that it is not possible to backslide, merely to stand still or progress. Therefore, the physical stage is for the purpose of advancing the progression of the soul through overcoming of temptation and assisting others to advance. If this is thoroughly understood, it will help to emphasize the importance of overcoming bad habits, silencing sharp tongues, quelling anger and pettiness, and putting the welfare of others at least on a par with one's own, so that no unkind deed or word passes from one soul aimed at another soul. In the spirit state we automatically assist others as needed, for we are directly under the laws of God and without as much personal choice as you there enjoy for a brief span of years. That is your most crucial testing. Do you make the most of it? Do you shed habits which delay progress and tie you too much to the earthbound state after coming into spirit form? Drinking, drugs, nicotine in all forms—these are habits to be broken there, so that they do not hold back your development in the next stage. Automatically learning to think of the welfare of others, putting forth love instead of an angry outburst, thinking how much we dislike being the object of another's wrath and then determining never again to make another person the object of ours; putting husband before self or wife before self; loving those whom it is difficult for you to love because they are on a different vibratory level from you—these are terribly important in the physical state. For on this side we automatically avoid those on different wavelengths or vibrations, since only like attraction brings us together: Thus, the importance of growth on that side, where the challenge exists."

Ford himself had by no means exhausted the subject. I flew to Indianapolis for a visit with my family, and the first day that I returned to the typewriter Arthur wrote, "Glad you had a nice trip. Now let us speak again of those who, having reached this stage beyond death, are unable to forget that they were humans with human desires of the flesh and will not adjust here because they are unable to break habits incurred during the physical life just past. They hover around those who smoke or drink or take drugs, trying to enjoy the fumes or sensations as they once did and anxious to be part of the group that is enjoying drinking, or inhaling drugs, or taking pot and the like. They are to those on this side very pathetic souls, for they are so attached to the habit that they will not let go of it, trying to enjoy nefariously what they still crave here. They are so intent on these pleasures that they do not begin to develop spiritually here for such a long time that it is a terrible setback to their souls' advancement.

"For this reason, if for no other, it is far better to break the smoking, drinking, or drug habits while in the flesh. It is easier by far to give them up there than it is to wait for the spirit life, when it is so nearly impossible to break the habit that one usually carries it back with him into the next earthly existence, when it may take a different and sometimes even more lethal form of intoxication or addiction."

I lacked the nerve to ask another direct question about his own addiction to alcohol, but one day Ford began abruptly, "Now let's discuss the question that has been bothering you—whether I continue to yearn for alcohol or other habits such as cigarettes and drugs. The answer is that if I had never touched them in the physical life just ended, I would be much better off here, with keener perceptions and more rapid development of soul. Yes, I sometimes hover around someone who is on a heavy bender, and this is a shameful and terrible thing, but there it is—a warning to others to lick the habit while there.

"You, Ruth, with your heavy smoking will not be able to shake it over here unless you first kick the habit there. I had never completely licked the problem with alcohol, as you know, falling off the wagon so to speak from time to time. Had I completely abandoned the bottle there and turned my attention to other things, I would be far better able to cope with advancement here, without that earthly tie in the wrong direction. So take heed. You know I'm not one for handing out unsolicited advice, but you did ask, and this is the answer. Abandon those habit-forming nuisances while you still can!"

# XII

# Between Earth Lives

Arthur Ford has followed no particular sequence in writing his contributions for this book. Some mornings are devoted to the subject of reincarnation, some to life in the higher states of being, and others to schools and behaviorism in the stage where he now is. Since we in physical bodies are accustomed to a more orderly progression, it has been necessary to sort these messages into categories, even though they sometimes overlap.

Often, in the middle of a serious discussion his pixie humor shines through with such suddenness that I can almost hear his familiar chuckle. Once when I was plying him with questions about famous personages in past ages, I inquired, "What is (blank) doing now?" I was trying to trick him, since he had previously told me that in one of my previous incarnations I had been that person, but he unhesitatingly replied, "You ought to know. Sitting at a typewriter asking me questions." Another day, when I asked how I could break the cigarette habit, he urbanely responded, "By not smoking."

Sometimes he gave amusing portrayals of souls whom we ordinarily think of as dead. On March 3 he wrote, "We grow, we live, we love, to return in endless cycles until at last we slough off the imperfections which we picked up along the way and are fit to become a part of

God Himself. Why are there so many sinners? Because so many of us put pleasure ahead of service It's as simple as that. If more of us found sheer pleasure in helping others, we would advance much more rapidly, because that would be combining business with pleasure. But the slothful, easy way is that most often followed: turning to idle pastimes and pursuits which are not helping others or even ourselves. That's what we are wont to call human nature, meaning the nature of a soul when occupying a physical form. The carnal lusts, the aimless dallying, the egotistical ways and pampering of self all help to make up what we think of as human nature. Yet some of it continues on this side, in the spirit form as well. Some primp before mirrors which their thought forms have created, wearing fancy clothing which they have wished into seeming reality. They lacquer hair which is only there in thought, live in fine homes created by their lust for importance, and drive such long automobiles that if we had to move out of the way of solid objects, we'd be dodging traffic all day long. But they are only thought forms, and thus are real only to those who believe in them. It sounds funny, but we are not able to chuckle much at this obsession with things which continues even over here, because any soul who lags behind is pulling at the entire human race, as souls of man are called. Remember that, Ruth. What each of us does that is wrong affects all the rest of us adversely, and progress for the whole of mankind is the important point to remember as necessary. That's why Christ said 'love one another,' and 'love thy neighbor as thyself.' So let's push onward and upward, all of us, giving everyone else an assist."

A week later came this message, "Let's discuss the way to prepare ourselves for the various stages of advancement. As we have stressed, the path is steep because it is necessary to help the others up the rising path too. For instance, if you try to press forward alone or race others toward the crest, you never reach the summit, because the ones left behind are pulling you backwards faster than you are able to climb. They need assistance, and for every stop along the way to take the hand of another, you are not losing ground but gaining it. That's another example of why time means nothing except as a way to time appointments in the physical state. Time is relative and on this side means nothing. Even where you are, time races only when you want it to go slowly or creeps when you wish that it would speed up. There is always time to help another. On this side we automatically help anyone who seems in need of our time. There is no question here of purely self-advancement. Instead we follow the laws of the universe, so apparent here, and realize that neglecting others is the primary way to backslide and have to start all over again.

"When we adapt ourselves to this new but age-old philosophy, we find happiness always present. No jealousies here, no pushing for position, no envy or malice. How would it be possible, when we are all one, to be jealous of another finger or toe? Are the hairs of our head jealous or envious of each other? No, they are all a part of the whole, as are your two eyes, your nose and ears. Each has an assigned duty, and not one of them is trying to outshine or outdo another part of your body. So it is with us, when we on this side realize the vast scope of God's plan. We are as one, some with totally different obligations than others, but pulling together to make a harmonious whole. So why not think along those lines while you are in physical form? Try to surround yourself with harmonious thoughts, not by pulling into a cocoon but by spreading harmony around you. If you pour forth warmth and love, the souls around you will feel the encompassing harmony and subconsciously want to be near you. Don't pull away. Give of self and extend a helping hand to any that are outstretched."

Stressing that this is the only way to advance spiritually, Ford continued, "Why bother then to learn pious phrases, to make a name for oneself in the arts or
135

sciences, when the progress which we all crave is measured only by how much you have helped another along the way? Here it is as nothing if a famous man steps through the door to our side. Why is he famous? Because he invented something for which the idea came from our side of the open door? Is he famous because he sang with perfect key and resonance? That was a talent bestowed on him by our Creator. It is whether these gifts were used to assist others and make their path brighter that weighs in his favor on this side. The point is, do I stop to assist with the burdens of others or am I too interested in my own brilliance? The tortoise and the hare, remember? The hare forgetting to help others, running by spurts and stops and thinking only of his own supremacy, while the tortoise plodded along, carrying a heavy load on his back."

Arthur never tired of discussing the types of schools which are available on his side of the grave. Once he wrote, "For those who are eager to push ahead with spiritual advancement, they will no sooner assess their previous lifetime in the physical body than they will register for further directions from a master. Each of us has special masters who have volunteered to help such souls grow and develop on this side. So they take the newcomer under their wing, so to speak, which is about as close as we get to wings over here. We meet for regular study, for here we automatically obey universal laws for orderly advancement. Otherwise chaos would result, since there are many more souls here than currently in your physical plane. Some are awaiting their turn to plunge again into physical form, while others are attempting to advance to higher planes. Until you and I have completed this current project, I will not need to decide my course.

"Now let's talk about the courses of study. No need for arithmetic or geometry here, because those are needed only in the physical plane. Spelling is passé. We think in universal symbols and need no words in this language or that. Reading is reserved only for those who wish to scan akashic records, which are of course in universal symbols. Writing is the same. We write nothing here, for the records called akashic are indelibly imprinted by a soul's deeds and thoughts rather than inscribed with pen and ink. So what do we study? The rudiments of science for some, particularly those who wish to project ideas to scientists on the earth plane. Philosophy, for those who want to comprehend more of the universal laws. Goodness, which is the philosophy of living one with another. Ecology, for it will be needed more and more to help those in physical form to salvage what remains of earth's environment for future returning souls. Love—yes, even that has to be learned, because so many of us unlearned it long ago in previous physical lives. Why would we need to study love? Because without love there is no harmony, and unless there is harmony the whole universal scheme of things will fall apart. Makes it a mighty important subject for study and discussion.

"We learn that love has little to do with physical attraction. That is an animal characteristic that arises from wearing physical form in the earth phase. Love is the attraction of soul for soul, and to enlarge the scope we need to file off our rough spots of personality, so that we are lovable to a larger and ever more expanding circle of souls. This is possible, you know. Souls which once avoided each other like poison ivy on earth become devoted partners here, after each has gone through this cleansing experience of smoothing out the rough spots of his manner and behavior and conduct. As more and more souls find themselves in harmony, the expanding circle imprints itself on the world in which you and we both live: fewer wars, more exchanges and sharing between peoples and nations. And it is reflected here. When turmoil is everywhere, you may be sure that it is reflected on both sides of the veil. Dissident souls avoiding and shunning each other have their effects on both sides of the veil."

The akashic records, Ford said, are those which we make with every deed and thought and act, "and the only way to erase the bad marks is to perform a kindly act for someone in need." For every good deed, he said, "we are also given a mark which is not jotted down by some scorekeeper but automatically impressed on the record by each soul. We keep our own books in that way, and we are our own judge and jury, for what we would like to think of as a harsh judgment by some gray-beard is simply our own conscience, from which there is no escape. This will always be with us, as it has always been, and from time immemorial we have been placing our stamp on our own scroll. This is an important point. No slipping one over on the teacher or scorekeeper. Cheating does no good. We are the ones who keep the score, and we are never able to fool ourselves."

Arthur stressed that the lessons learned in spirit schools are absorbed through a kind of osmosis. "The masters are here for those of us who want to drive more deeply into the laws of phenomena as manifested in the physical earth. We use them here to project our thoughts to those of you there who are interested in advancing your own knowledge of cosmic truths. Those who warn of danger in this pursuit [of esoteric knowledge] should understand that some have the ability developed in ages past to communicate easily with those on the other side of the thin veil between these two stages of continued life, and if balance is present, no dangers exist. The lack of a balanced personality will evoke problems whether one tries to communicate or lulls himself with belief in angels with harps. The unbalance is the lurking danger. Why would it be less dangerous to meditate on angels than on souls who have passed from the physical into the spirit world? As your father once told you, Ruth, those who go off their nuts trying to delve into this field would have gone off their rockers in some other endeavor instead. There are plenty of imbalanced persons whose personalities have not knit securely, and through no fault of the occult their personalities seem at times to split apart."

Returning to the subject of spirit schools, he said,

"There are those souls who, having lived a full life in the earth phase, are in no rush to return. These take up studies here which will benefit other souls both here and in the flesh. They want to know how a child in the physical phase will better be able to withstand temptations and illnesses and accidents, so they do a great deal of research here. They work through scientists and psychologists and doctors still in physical body to bring these advancements to them. They are often able to inject these notions and suggestions into their minds through waking, as well as dream state: a sudden inspiration which leads to a breakthrough, a deft placing of a new instrument or book at their elbow, an insinuation into the conscious mind as well as through the subconscious while in drowsy or sleeping state.

"Most of the breakthroughs in the earthly state originated with souls working on the problem here, where we have wider grasp of the problems and the solutions. As I said, this is a busy, working world where I am now. What of those who invent evil tools for destruction? That too often originates on this side where I am, but the utilization which turned a good idea into a destructive purpose came from the physical bodies and not from the spirit souls. Any invention has the potential of good or evil, depending upon who puts it to use, and it is a pity that marvelous scientific breakthroughs so often fall into the wrong brains and hands and are distorted into evil use rather than developed for the advancement of all mankind. Take the rioters and protestors. What a wonderful good they would do if they provided the solutions, instead of breaking down the good along with the bad in the system which they so loudly protest."

# XIII

## Examples of Reincarnation

The morning of Good Friday, Arthur Ford wrote on my typewriter: "On this approximate date nearly two thousand years ago, a man named Jesus who came from Nazareth died on the cross as a living symbol of eternal life. Some thought that He would remove himself from the cross to exhibit another miracle, but it was the Christ within him that survived death and returned again and again in astral form to prove that life is eternal, that the man of flesh is not the true man, but merely the physical symbol of the ever-living soul. He proved the truth of His preaching, and thereby became immortal as a physical Jesus as well as of the Christ consciousness, which has existed in the forces of God from the beginning of time.

"Now let's take the case of Saint Paul, who saw a vision of Christ on the road to Damascus. He had never known the man Jesus, but instantly he saw the apparition he recognized it as the Christ who had inhabited the body of Jesus. The words to him were unmistakable. Jesus was the greatest of a long line of embodiments of one soul created in the beginning and from time to time incarnating in human form. He was the Buddha, the Messiah, the all-in-all, and the one for whom we always yearn within our soul—the big brother, the good guy, the peacemaker, the embodiment of good. God's son, to be sure, but aren't we all sons and daughters of God? The difference is that Jesus was empowered by God to lead all mankind back to basic truths: love one another, be good to those who harm you, speak no ill unless you want to be spoken ill of, do unto others as you would have others do unto you. The Christ Spirit lived and had its being for a span of years within Jesus of Nazareth, but remember this: The indwelling spirit which inhabits the physical form of all of us is equally a part of God and capable of withstanding evil, so let us each try a little harder to be that which in the beginning was pure and clean and true. Love thy neighbor as thyself."

Arthur carried forward a similar theme in his Easter morning "sermon," writing, "Today marks the anniversary of the beautiful morning when the disembodied Christ arose from the tomb to demonstrate life eternal. Freed from his body, he appeared to many of his followers throughout the Palestinian land and even showed his wounds to doubting Thomas, but this is not the important message. The salient point is that we all survive death with personality and memory intact. This Jesus demonstrated by dying on the cross, and the eternal part of Him—the Christ—lived on to prove that the physical body is not a part of the everlasting soul. Today we speak of the various incarnations of that Christ whom we remember in the form of Jesus. He had been a number of different men before that incarnation and in all of them was seeking the perfection of man. He wished to demonstrate to His Father and all others that it is possible to inhabit a physical body, withstand temptation, and live a life of perfection. Sometimes we forget that Jesus was a man like the rest of us. It was the Christ within that made Him superior. The same fleshly temptations were there to taunt Jesus as any other living man in the flesh, yet he withstood them all. Let us remember then that each of us will be able to live as righteously as he wants, because it has been demonstrated that man even in the flesh is able to be perfect."

Continuing, he said, "Now let's take the case of a man who tries to perfect himself in one lifetime in the flesh, but who has so much previous karma to resolve that the task seems impossible. 'Is it impossible?' you ask. Yes and no, for if the previous karma is sufficiently bad he will still have to make amends within himself, but by forgiving all others and then forgiving himself, he will come under the law of grace which wipes out past sins when truly repentant. This is the holy spirit which Jesus of Nazareth announced would come after him. Make use of this holy spirit of grace, and remember that to become involved with it, it is necessary not only to forgive others but also ourselves. 'Love' is the key word. Love others as well as oneself, but also learn to love oneself."

During my preparation for writing *Here and Hereafter*, I seemed to relive a number of previous lives while under prenatal hypnotic regression. Two of them seem worthy of relating here because subsequent events have lent credence to what I "saw" during hypnosis. In one, I found myself sitting in the lotus position at an ashram in the lower Himalayas. My arms were small and dark. Under questioning I described our diet at the ashram—berries, fruits, and nuts—and I said that I was a guru for young boys who came up from the village below, but that I also studied with a more advanced guru who lived higher up the mountain.

The hypnotist (the woman scientist whom I called Jane Winthrop in *Here and Hereafter*) then took me forward twenty-five years and asked if I was still in the same ashram. I looked about in perplexity, and then came understanding. My higher guru had passed on, I explained, and I had taken over his duties. Jane asked if I had a mantram, and I exclaimed, "Certainly, everyone has a mantram." Told to give mine, I burst forth in a cadence I had never knowingly heard before, melding two syllables over and over.

I told no one of this experience, for obvious reasons. The possibility seemed too remote for further consideration. Two months later, a stranger came to my house in Virginia Beach and introduced himself as Dr. I. C. Sharma of Udaipur, India, who was then an exchange professor of philosophy at a small university in Virginia. He had read my psychic books and wanted to discuss the subject with me. As he was preparing to leave, I expressed the wish to know what my mantram was, since each soul is supposed to have an individual vibration with God, and he said that he would meditate on mine.

Two weeks later he returned to Virginia Beach for another visit, bringing his wife, and when they prepared to depart I rather wistfully said, "I suppose you haven't had time to meditate on my mantram."

"Indeed I have," Dr. Sharma replied, "I will write it for you here." He handed me a slip of paper on which were two syllables written as one, and to my astonishment they were exactly the same as those I had repeatedly uttered while under hypnosis. Needless to say, I have since used that mantram in my daily meditation.

I repeat that story here because during a discussion of reincarnation the spirit of Arthur Ford wrote, "You were once a guru in India in the Himalayas, and I knew you in that incarnation, for I was then your guru and you studied with me until I passed on into the spirit plane. Then you succeeded to my post. You were a worthy student and we were exceedingly fond of each other, you as a lad and I as an old man then."

In repeating my second "past life" experience, I feel some embarrassment, but perhaps it will encourage others to delve into their own subconscious memories. This seeming recall began five years ago when, during meditation, I saw myself as a little girl of five or six years watching some Wise Men arrive not far from our cottage in Bethlehem. I knew that a baby had been born nearby, and sometime later I begged my father to let me follow the crowd to watch the baby being bathed in a pool somewhere between Bethlehem and Jerusalem. He at first demurred, but I pleaded so desperately that at last we started down the road, and as I slipped my little hand into his, I knew that he was the same soul as Arthur Ford.

During the next day's meditation I saw myself as a woman who had just heard that the baby, now grown to manhood, was preaching near the Dead Sea. I yearned to hear him, but because my husband would not give consent for me to go I raced across the desert, leaving my young baby behind. Later, under hypnosis by Jane Winthrop, I relived some of this. I caught up with the crowd surrounding Jesus in the desert and became one of his large group of followers. Then, sitting with Him at a house in Bethany, I realized that I was a sister of Lazarus, but I knew that I was neither Mary nor Martha, because both of them were also present.

This seemed too ridiculous for further contemplation, so I kept it to myself. Yet one of the first fan letters I received after publication of *Here and Hereafter* came from an unknown reader who said that he had psychically received the impression that I had once been a sister of Lazarus. Another few weeks passed, and one day on impulse I bought a copy of the book *The Aquarian Gospel of Jesus the Christ,* which had been psychically received at the beginning of the century by a man who identified himself only as Levi. Because it was written in Biblical style, I read only small portions each day; but great was my bafflement when I stumbled across a passage which discussed Lazarus and his *three* sisters— Martha, Mary, and Ruth. Thereafter, in various references to this third sister, who is not mentioned in the Bible, Levi said that she had deserted her husband and two children to follow Jesus because her husband had no sympathy for the movement. He said that Jesus eventually persuaded Ruth to return to her family, and that after she did so her husband became converted and both were then active among His followers.

On March 7, 1971, Arthur Ford wrote on my typewriter, "You are eager to know about my previous lives in connection with your own. I am able to remember some of that, at least those which affected most directly my life as Arthur Ford. In one I was a Buddhist monk in Thailand, and I was a Dominican monk in another life, somewhere in France. These were not too many lives ago. I was also the father of a little girl named Ruth in the Holy Land, and also of Mary, Martha, and Lazarus. That was a strenuous but exalting life, even though I did not make full use of my potential there by becoming a priest for Jesus. But I was considerably older than Jesus and was no longer living when He met His death on the cross. You were a child when he was born, and so were some of my other children. Some were older and some younger than you. We moved from Bethlehem to Bethany, but not long after that I passed on, leaving son Lazarus in charge.

"Lazarus was not buried alive but did indeed die and come back to life, regardless of what the scoffers say. I was with him on this side and then watched as he returned to the physical body to prove that such things are possible if God wishes them to be done. I am glad no one called me back this time, as I am much happier in the spirit than the flesh, at least the flesh I had this last time around. You were not as obedient as Martha and even Mary. You ran off from your husband because he would not drop everything to follow Jesus. You had to have your own way then as now, and you returned to your family only after Jesus himself persuaded you to put aside your impetuosity and put family first. This lesson is still a hard one for you to learn, Ruth, because you seem always to put the I before the We or You. Try to overcome this tendency, or you'll be forever making high resolutions and then returning to the physical cycle to make the same mistakes over again."

Arthur then gave me a bit of stern preaching about putting We and You before Me, adding, "Hand the reins to Bob for a while and learn to be a Japanese wife, following along behind him and letting him run the show for a while. It's a lesson in humility for you and also a test of grace." He made my face burn, because I knew that he had put his finger on one of my worst faults. I love to be the leader!

In April, during one of our typewriter sessions, I asked Arthur if he could tell me anything more about our Palestinian life, and he responded, "It is as you already know—you the sister of Lazarus and I the father of the brood. We were not quite as high-minded as Lazarus and Mary and Martha, so they left us out of the Good Book, which will always be a regret, for we had the same opportunities as the others did but failed to make the most of them. I was not a follower of Jesus, for his preaching began after I had passed on, but the opportunity of service was there for me, and I feel that I failed to make the most use of it, being as I was a rather conservative Jew who was more interested in rote than right.

"You were a delightful daughter and my favorite of the children, but you put yourself ahead of your husband and children and therefore missed the opportunity for greater service. It is true that you yearned to be a follower of the man Jesus who was the Christ, but instead of following Him around to hear Him speak and feast on His wise words, you would have been better off to concern yourself with the welfare of your children. Jesus knew this, of course, and finally sent you back home, and there you did your best work in gradually converting your husband to His teachings, and toward the last of Jesus' life there you were both followers along with your little children."

Arthur has, of course, written about numerous other lives of mine and his and of our previous contacts with some of the relatives and friends now living, but since hopefully this is a book of general interest, these others need not be included here. One day I asked how we determine which race and geographical location to choose when we decide to reincarnate, and he said, "This really provides one of the most sensitive problems, for where we will best meet ourselves to work out past karma and

146

develop higher qualities of character is all-embracing. Will we meet ourselves better if, having been an intolerant, bigoted person toward minority groups such as blacks or Jews, we become one of that race or nationality the next time around? This is often the case, and some of those Negroes who are in the forefront of the civil rights movements were formerly white slaveowners who proved so intolerant toward the human rights of their slaves or minions that they took this opportunity of becoming themselves black, so that they were able to help their people from within, rather than try to uplift from without.

"Some of the Jews who died during the Hitler regime were formerly those who had persecuted Jews in previous witchhunts and who had voluntarily come back as Jews in order to right their wrongs. They paid the supreme penalty by losing their lives but in doing so aroused the conscience of mankind and therefore advanced spiritually by many leaps and bounds. This was also race karma, for the Old Testament itself sometimes depicts the Jews of old as a warlike race that subjugated others in the name of its religion. Thus, we find that both race karma and individual karma were being met at that time, which does not excuse Hitler and his lieutenants one iota. They will be paying for their transgressions for many hundreds or perhaps thousands of years, so that judgment is not ours to make.

"Each of us meets self both in the flesh and in this more normal spirit plane, and we are our own harshest judge. The sins which we like to think are so perilous in the flesh phase are seldom the real ones when viewed on this side. We ask ourselves, Whom did we harm through our actions? Were they for self-aggrandizement and fleshly pleasure, or were we actually thinking of someone else and not wishing to harm that person? Self-denial is one of the greatest virtues, because it teaches us to put the love of others before love of self. Discipline is good for the soul. We need it all the time, but here we have so little opportunity for practicing it that we return again and again to the flesh in order to wipe out our self-indulgences and practice self-denial."

In commenting on our failure to recall past lives, Ford wrote, "For the most part we bring with us into the physical mind some memories of this spirit life and sometimes even flashes of memories of former earth lives—mostly if we have willed ourselves to do so and are determined to continue on the same path that we pursued in an earlier incarnation. These thoughts influence our actions and thoughts while we are there, and flashbacks often come during dreaming, when we are in a suspended state of physical activity. These dreams are often links with the past, and if we paid heed to them we would find it easier to progress. They are not disjointed hallucinations but a steady stream of consciousness which stays with us throughout eternity, or until the past errors are eventually wiped out by subsequent acts which make amends. We, like you, are striving to perfect the soul. We see souls so transformed by goodness that we yearn to model ourselves after them. Yet aping another is not the way to rise and shine. Within each soul is the knowledge of good and evil, and each of us is affected differently by temptations and kindnesses. Thus, although we are all a part of the Supreme Whole, yet we are as different as fingerprints one from another. Just as a toe serves a different function from a finger, so we each have our own roles and must find our own path to perfection. A knuckle joint should not try to imitate a nose, and so it is with us. We know what is right, so why not do it?"

Still fascinated by Arthur's earlier discussion of the "heavenly computers" which select candidates for reentry into physical form, I asked him for further elaboration, and he wrote, "To begin with, the time between lives in physical body can be a thousand or a hundred years by earth reckoning, or a few hours or days or weeks or years. Some need desperately to make amends, and some who are tired of earthly woes want a long period of resting. Either way, he will not be able totally to decide for himself when he will return to the flesh, because other elements enter into the decision. For instance, there are only so many opportunities to return to a woman who wishes to be a mother. Since there are others waiting their opportunity, a system exists for rationing the mothers, so to speak, among the souls wanting to be reborn. The system goes into effect each time that a woman conceives.

"If she herself is a lofty soul who deserves the right to have a lofty soul to rear as her flesh child, she will be given higher priority than one who thinks only of carnal pleasure. For these superior souls a system of classification will be set up here, so that those who qualify may be given a testing period to determine who is best qualified to meet the needs of the physical parents and also to fulfill his own goals. These are processed through what in your realm might be called a computer, but here it is an automatic processing that furnishes all data concerning parents and the soul wanting to reincarnate. Seldom is there any question about who will best serve his purpose in that particular earth cycle, for no two souls are alike. Those who have previously known or loved the two souls who are about to become parents will be given first priority if they have karmic problems to work out with that particular couple.

"The fortunate soul who wins the right enters that fetus at or near the time of physical birth, while the other candidates search for other opportunities until one that matches their goal again becomes available and their numbers come up, so to speak. Those who are not so highly evolved or have greater karmic debts to repay will have to settle for less attractive situations, and some will gladly be born into ghettos or backward nations in order to learn humility or suffering, with the firm resolve to overcome these obstacles and achieve higher status as more advanced spiritual beings. Let me emphasize that no one is forced to return to physical form. If we so choose, we are permitted to remain here throughout eternity, although it is harder to advance. But those who rush back to physical bodies too quickly, settling for any opportunity that becomes available, have a difficult time in the earth cycle, for they learned little while here and did not properly assess the purpose of another physical round. Thus we have the many maimed and crippled beggars, and even thieves and robbers, who would not wait for appropriate physical form but seized any vehicle in sight."

At one point, when Arthur was discussing a young mother who died in her prime, leaving a large family of children behind, I asked what this had to do with karma. He replied, "Take one example at a time. Let's say that in another lifetime this selfsame mother deserted her children by running off with another man. In this last life she had to pay the penalty by leaving children when her heart was full of love for them. This was her way, her soul's way, of balancing the ledger. But what of the children left behind? Perhaps they too in a previous life had scorned supervision, going their headstrong ways and rebelling at kindly parental discipline. In this last life they loved their mother devotedly but were forced to do without her when she crossed over to this side. The law of karma is inexorable, unless through true repentance we are able to overcome some measure of it with the grace of God.

"This example is not, of course, true of all such cases. Sometimes a mother has simply overburdened herself with too much childbearing and passion, and her physical temple is not sturdy enough to withstand the pressures. Sometimes an accident takes her away during her prime, but when this occurs there is usually a karmic basis, such as having lacked sympathy for a struggling young mother in a previous life or having abused her body in that life to the point that it will not stand up to the present pressures. Suppose this mother in a previous life had deliberately taken the life of another. In this one, the life that is taken is her own. A gloomy subject to dwell upon, although a necessary lesson to learn."

Another day he wrote, "What of mother-child relationships? Why are some mothers so close to their children and so adored by them, while with others the friction is constant? One has chosen because of strong ties of love to be born to that woman, while the other has agreed to work on karma by coming to a former rival, enemy, or total stranger with whom he has nothing in common.

"All right. How does this knowledge prepare you for coming over here in what you call old age? 'Going home,' says the psalm. True. We *are* at home on this side. It is there that we have made the adventure and stepped forth into alien ways, risking all for a chance to advance spiritually. The bright promises that are made here, the determined resolutions to advance quickly and be undeterred by earth's forces and temptations are beautiful to see. Alas, the souls drag themselves back here more often than not in anguished defeat, realizing that what they had pledged to do was not fulfilled. At first they try to blame it on circumstances or on another person who blocked their progress, but as time passes and the soul devotes itself to earnest meditation on this side, it comes to realize that it was himself, the old fogie self, who caused the trouble.

"So what to do? Resolve to review every mistake frankly while still there in the body physical. Review as earnestly there as you will be sure to do on this side. But make the review there, while there is still opportunity to change the direction of the pathway and mount to loftier heights. On this side all that a soul is able to do is review, assess, study, resolve, and prepare for the next go-round in the body physical. There you still have ample opportunity to fulfill the original mission, or at least to light the path of another, which earns you extra bonus stamps to trade in on faith."

Lily then broke in to say, "How do we overcome temptations of the flesh and grow in depth? By listening to the still small voice within."

# XIV

## Higher Planes and
## Other Planets

From time to time when referring to Edgar Cayce, Yogananda, Betty White, and other highly evolved souls,
Arthur Ford made tantalizingly brief references to
"higher planes" and "other planets." On April 10 I
asked for greater elaboration, and he wrote, "The higher
planes that you ask about are essentially higher degrees
of consciousness. In other words, the place is similar,
but the level of consciousness is so much more rarefied
that those on this plane cannot advance into them without great preparation, whereas those on some of the
higher planes encounter no difficulty in living in our plane
simultaneously. It is a bit like the difference between our
state and yours. Those in the next higher state are
more aware of us than we are of them. They progress
to that state when their rough, earthbound edges are
rounded off, and their mental and spiritual progression is
such that they are ready for higher learning in the esoteric
sense. Those who feel that their progress will be more
rapid by assuming again an earthly identity seldom pass
on to that next higher stage, for to do so takes them
out of direct line for return to physical form."

Recalling that Arthur had made reference to a period
which he spent in a higher plane before returning here as
Arthur Ford, I asked if he and Lily were familiar with

that stage. "Yes," he replied, "and Lily spends much of his time in the higher frequency of that plane. He will not be able to tell you much about it, because there is little to record that you would be able to understand with a finite mind. As said previously, it is a higher consciousness rather than a different plane, for the universe is one. He will probably not return to another incarnation in the physical plane, although that choice for him remains.

"He was a writer in his last incarnation, and since there are many writers now, he needs to advance his growth here in work that many others are not able to do, such as counseling those writers who are progressing here and working directly with those in physical body who would write spiritual treatises of a higher order. To describe the difference in levels of consciousness is almost impossible to put into words, but let us think for a moment of a balloon filled with helium gas. On the ground it is a great physical form for all to see and touch, but when the moorings are cut it rises free of earth ties, which would correspond to the silver cord which at death releases a soul from the physical body. The balloon rises higher and higher until it reaches the thin stratosphere, and still it is as alive and touchable as when it was on earth, but man is no longer able from the earth to see or feel it. It passes from human sight and soars heavenward, but although gone from the immediate comprehension of man, it is still alive. After a time it loses all contact with the earth, and although the balloon is fully aware of what is going on below because of its memory and intelligence, those on earth no longer have contact with it. This is a poor analysis, but it is hard to explain in terms understood by the finite mind.

"In this higher consciousness the soul of man is as alive and aware as ever it was in physical form but is totally detached from the ties of physical form. We are now in the intermediate state, with earth ties and tensions, but when Lily goes into the higher state of consciousness

153

he relinquishes all pulls from physical wills and barriers."

I broke in to ask what Edgar Cayce meant by saying that a soul between lives sometimes goes to Uranus or other planets in consciousness, and he replied, "Many of the planets are occupied by spirit forms in various states of consciousness. Some are in higher and some in lower forms of consciousness than the earth dwellers, but because of various levels of development, some evolve more rapidly in certain vibratory planes than in others. Thus, some may visit for a time in Venus or Uranus or Mars or other planets. The communications which occasionally seem to be picked up from other planets are thought forms which they are able to send out in vibrations usually too high for your instruments to record. But occasionally, under certain atmospheric conditions of low enough caliber, your finest instruments are affected by them."

Another day Ford said of the higher states, "From my own recollections I am able to say that the work there is of a different type, for instead of helping new souls to come over and learning lessons in philosophy, the advanced soul will be testing these theories and proving them as fact, while also taking on such interesting assignments as visiting other planets where forms of life exist and relating them to our own system from whence all of us here were once a part.

"The Atlanteans (those from the lost continent of Atlantis), many of whom were of a high order of development, often inhabit other planes and planets while taking note of that which is occurring in the earth, for parts of Atlantis will be more plainly seen within a decade, as the land once again rises toward the surface. These Atlanteans are keen on proving that they were of a superior order, and that the human race will be able to recapture some of its esoteric knowledge during the Aquarian Age now at hand. Needless to say, many of these Atlanteans have reincarnated again and again in physical form, and you and I were once Atlanteans ourselves, although some who have not returned to the physical are of exceedingly high vibration and were what we might term princes among men. They are so high in the order of superior beings as not to need further earth returns, although some of them are keen to do it when Atlantis rises, for there is tremendous interest in leading the world to hiding places where material of towering worth is stored, safe from disintegration. Meanwhile, they have been instructing those souls who advance beyond this stage where I now am and are helping them to understand the mysteries of the universe—those mysteries which souls inhabiting the world once knew automatically."

One week later Ford announced that Lily would personally discuss the higher states of being, and Lily promptly wrote, "As we learn our lessons here in this intermediate state, we are given the choice of reincarnating or traveling onward to other realms of consciousness, and some of us elect to take this next step, as I have here. When we are ready, by having completed our philosophic discussions and reassessing our errors of flesh, we feel a lightening of spirit and with a little effort of thought are able to lift ourselves into a new consciousness in which we lose contact for a time with those here and those in your physical state of being.

"We then find ourselves in what would be thought of as a purely ethereal realm, with total loss of contact with other souls for a time. This is a somewhat lonely experience, since we are used to having shared thoughts and ideas here as well as in the physical body. After a time we seem to float into what, for want of a better term, would be called outer space but is such high frequency that there is no way to put it into words that are understandable to physical man. We are, let us say, in the realm of Uranus, where vibrations are so tremendous that at first we feel shaken to our core. It is a violent atmosphere, or rather lack of atmosphere, where there is no protection from the rays and beams and pulsations. We stay there, if we are able to endure it, for a time while preparing for still another step in our development.

"Later we may pass on to Venus or Mars, or any of the other realms of consciousness in our planetary group. We are not so much a part of that planet as we are under the influence of its vibrations. We walk on the surfaces of these planets much as you in the physical state walk on earth, except that our beta bodies have no weight and no embodiments of flesh. We are rather more like ideas, and since we see other souls of like covering there, we could be said to mingle with them, but only as ideas. Some of the planetary vibrations are gentle and soothing, and others fiery and full of antagonistic pulls and pushes. We need to experience all of these in order to understand the universal oneness of all mankind and the laws which govern us."

The next morning the writing began, "Ruth, this is Lily and the group, with Art participating. We are eager to tell you more about what occurs as the soul advances from this intermediate stage from which we are communicating with you. In the higher state this two-way communication is impossible, except for some such soul on the earth plane as Edgar Cayce, who was able so to step up his vibrations that by lowering our vibrations we could meet him halfway, so to speak. When I wish to summon the talents of one with whom we would commune, I return from the higher to this intermediate state, but that is why I do not hang around you all the time waiting until your highness is ready to be seated and receive. I am not trying to be sarcastic [Oh, no? I thought to myself] but merely to explain that there are many things more pressing than waiting around to see if you arise and shine in time for these morning sessions.

"In the next phase where I spend most of my life I am transfigured, so to speak, wearing light rather than astral form. This is because of the intensity of our devotion to the work of the Creator, and since we slip easily from the vibrations of one planet to others, we are best fitted for that work as a beam of light. Whatever form we wear, we never cease to be our own ego, for the self is what we will never escape. Some may wonder why there are those highly evolved souls in the earth plane who are always kindly and thoughtful, always willing to lend a helping hand, intelligent, beautiful, kings among men, while other souls are scarcely above the animal kingdom in their greediness, boorish manners, and lack of consideration for others. You wonder if each must always be himself throughout all the ages. The answer is yes, and before you think that this is unfair, I add that they started in the beginning as equal sparks of God. But as lives in the earth and on this side passed in succession, each developed his own personality through reaction to given situations, and since we choose our own situations into which to be born in the earth, they are the products of what they themselves have carried with them from one life to another in the earth plane. Interesting, isn't it! Each a duplicate of the other in the beginning, perfect sparks of God's love; yet how the earth plane changes them! This represents the reaction to temptation, so if one would be as the Master rather than as the uncouth oaf, let him look to himself and assess how he reacts to temptation. Form no habits that you cannot easily break, respond to the needs of others when asked, and remember always to be God-centered."

On May Day they went into greater detail about the advancing states, writing, "From here, as you know, we have the choice of returning to flesh or going on to what you would call the third stage and the fourth. These are not too different one from the other, except that in stage three the higher vibrations are mastered and the steps taken for mounting into still higher frequencies of what you would call sound and light. We here are able through antennalike adjustments to attune ourselves to waves of sound and light that would electrocute or permanently deafen the physical man. We are attuned to these higher forces through a thinness of radiation which no longer requires protection when in the spirit body. As we attune to these higher frequencies, we find ourselves in a state

157

most nearly described as fluid, for although there is no liquid, we are poured into the universal pattern, so to speak, and become so nearly one with it that we for a time lose consciousness of ego or self. We are a part of the fluid whole, and this benefits our understanding of what I have told you earlier about the realizations here that we are all a part of the perfect Whole.

"Now that is stage three, and stage four is what I have suggested in earlier reports: inhabitation of such other planets as Mars, Jupiter, Uranus, Venus, and the like, but not so much in a physical sense as in a state of higher consciousness; for while these planets contain life forms, they are totally unrecognizable in terms of the life forms which inhabit earth in physical form. These planets, each so different from one another, have various stages of development from the lowest protoplasm to the highest forms of thought patterns, and while Uranus is a particularly destructive planet in terms of reformation from evil, the most highly developed one is Saturn, which contains pure thoughts without embroilment in lower states of consciousness. Those who inhabit these planets for a time in thought form are sometimes so far removed from what earth folks call sanity and reason that if they ever decide thereafter to return to physical body they are rather out of tune with fellow souls incarnated at that time. Either they have mellowed to such an extent that they do not seem to have things in common with fellow souls there or they have been so fed by hatreds and warlike tendencies on Mars and some others that they are too antagonistic for comfortable living in the flesh."

At this point Arthur Ford broke in to say, "During my present time in this stage where I am now, I have not visited the other planets, but from recall I know of having been on three of them between other earth lives. I do not yet know whether I will go there again or will return to earth to complete my cycle of incarnations, but this I know: I do not want to visit Uranus again."

I asked Lily, Arthur, and the group whether any other planets are inhabited by physical forms somewhat similar to these on earth, and the reply was, "No, not life as we recognize it in the flesh form of earth. They have many species of interesting thought forms, such as radishes with wings, turnips with tails, lettuce that laughs, and animal forms which walk on air as well as water, besides many grotesque shapes of mineral life which would frighten an earthling out of his wits but which are quite as matter-of-fact there as river stones. They all have various forms of communication and operate on higher or lower frequencies than earth forms. They have their cycles of return to their planets, just as we reincarnate on earth, and once in a while the more adventuresome ones choose to tackle an earth life, but usually with disastrous results. For instance, when an aborigine is found in an isolated spot in Africa or wherever, he is usually one of these other-planet peoples trying to inhabit an earth body in the flesh. The little ones who occasionally have lived with animals and are unable to speak like a human when found are from other planets and through curiosity have tried out this new type of body. But they do not fit into it anymore than a wolf would wear sheep's clothing well.

"There are earth people who have tried guises of Saturn and other planets too, but the results are not beneficial. For instance, it is the same folly as trying to breed disparate animals one to another. When I say that we visit other planets for a time, I do not mean that we inhabit bodies there, as does the original life stock of those planets. We go simply as thought forms, to learn the laws of the universe and understand the immutability of the Law of One."

Another day they wrote, "These other stars present entirely different opportunities for growth than does the planet known as earth, the only one with which most of us are familiar here in this intermediate phase. We are all earth-trained souls. While we have recently come from

159

the physical earth phase, there are countless other souls who have developed while on other planets throughout the firmament. Some are purely spiritual habitations where the souls clothe themselves in thought rather than physical form. Some of the stars are habitable for physical form, but the souls there are not necessarily in physical form as we know it on the planet earth. The physical form assumed by a soul is compatible with environment, whether here, or on earth, or on other planets. Thus, what is suitable for one star often is not suitable for development on another.

"We think of man as having two eyes, two ears, a nose, a throat, legs, arms, and trunk, but this is not the sole way that a soul will project himself as he returns to different forms to complete his spiritual growth. This is the earth form, yes, but not necessarily the one for Mars or Saturn, or any of a vast firmament of stars. We when in flesh had lungs for breathing and a pump to keep us functioning, but such a heart and lungs are not necessary on some planets. A much simpler or more complex mechanism is necessary in some planets to sustain the activity of movement and thinking and being.

"Those souls who habitate other planets and stars are in various stages of development, some more primitive and some more advanced, but all are souls with the pulse of God within and the light of His love. Each has a responsibility for growth and correction of previous faults of the spirit to amend before he will be able to resume his journey toward reunion with the Creator.

"What if one soul goes astray on the earth to such a dire degree that it could take a thousand million lifetimes to undo that wrong which he has perpetrated on fellow souls? Sometimes in order to speed up the retribution he is given an opportunity to assume a totally different form of being on a harsher planet or star. There the conditions are such that, like a freshly created soul without sin, he will be able, if he perseveres under harsh surroundings, to develop enough atonement to make up for many lifetimes of mistake in the less severe habitat we know as earth. Am I making this clear? The soul who has lost hope of ever atoning for transgressions in the earth phase will volunteer to become an inhabitant of a harsher planet and to assume a guise which you of the earth would not consider human.

"Some souls have always lived and died, so to speak, on other stars and planets and have had no reason to think that such beings as we were existed in what we think of as human form. Again there are planets where souls exist only in the thought plane as true spirit, without physical bodies. Sometimes these are on a far higher plane of development than the souls we meet on earth in bodily form.

"Former earth beings who elect to go on to higher stages are as carefully schooled as if that soul were entering a monastery in the physical plane. They learn to project themselves through vibration into spheres they have sometimes not previously explored, and in this sense they become travelers not just in astral bodies, where they sometimes are seen by sensitive people in the physical realm, but also to other planets, as we have remarked earlier. This travel contributes much to their knowledge of universal laws, and when they are in the fourth or fifth stages they may often be seen simultaneously in several planets at the same time, for the soul in higher consciousness is able to project its image simultaneously in many directions.

"Now let's talk about the ultimate on this side of the veil, the highest perfection, when souls at last meld with God in perfect union. Obviously we here are yet to experience that bliss, but there is a teaching here that when souls near that final perfection they once again review not only their past lives but every thought and concept and idea which has touched them, or they it, since the beginning of the life of all of us. This is during the sixth plane. They finally decide that no stone remains unturned that they have not repaid in some manner or thought or

161

way, and that they therefore have atoned for misdeeds and are ready to join God. There is no conceit in this decision but a totally accurate assessment of life since the beginning. They then are drawn into the oneness of God in perfect peace. This is hearsay, of course, as those souls will never return or resume the wheel of destiny when that perfect moment comes."

After such a sublime discussion of oneness with God, it seemed ridiculous to ask about flying saucers, but I knew that if I did not do so, my readers would ask me. Ford, always agreeable, replied, "Yes, there are flying saucers and they do originate in the thoughts of those on other planets, but the physical manifestations which earth people seem to think they have touched or visited do not exist. They are not solids in the earthly sense, but transmissions of light and sound which appear as real as if they were made of steel. They are visible under certain conditions and have sometimes scorched the earth when venturing too near, but they are not available for entry by human beings in the earth plane." And that was that!

# XV

## Prophecy

During a lengthy discussion of time, early in March, Arthur Ford wrote, "Time has no meaning on this plane where I am now, because we realize that we are forever, without beginning or ending. Thus, time is nonexistent here, whereas in the earth phase the necessity of time is obvious to regulate sleep and awakening, birth and so-called death, and the orderly procession of one's workaday appointments." Then he wrote this tantalizing bit: "We see a much longer spectrum of time from this side of the veil than do you, but by no means do we see from the beginning to the end of life. We are no more infallible here than there, except for broader vision and deeper awareness of the purpose of God's plan.

"When we are born into the physical state, we are reduced to the pinpoint of so-called time and see no further ahead than the nursing or feeding, which is all that we need to know while a baby in arms. This pinpoint ever so gradually extends as babyhood becomes childhood, and on through the cycles of life there. At first time seems to drag as a child views the vast extension until some happy or dread event occurs, such as a party or the opening of school. To him it is a long time in relation to the span of physical life that he has lived to that point. But as we approach old age, time flees so rapidly that a year seems as a day to the little child. This is in proportion to the time spent in the physical body."

I was so intrigued by his assertion that on his plane souls see "a longer spectrum of time" that I asked if he could prophesy some coming events. He had already indicated that the lost continent of Atlantis would become visible during the next decade and that our active participation in Vietnam was drawing rapidly toward a close. But there were other things I wished to know, and I remembered that Fletcher had proven to be an excellent prognosticator when he spoke through the entranced Ford. A year before President Kennedy's assassination, Fletcher told me during a sitting that Jack would be killed in a moving conveyance while away from the White House. A week before the 1964 election, on October 28, during a sitting in Philadelphia, Fletcher introduced the late Harold Ickes, who had been FDR's Secretary of the Interior, and said, "Ickes predicts that the Goldwater electoral vote will be a minimum of forty-three and a maximum of fifty-two." The Goldwater electoral vote turned out to be fifty-two. Fletcher also made such an accurate prediction about my sister Margaret that when the totally unexpected event shortly transpired, it gave me the creeps.

Therefore, for what they are worth, I now disclose the predictions that Arthur Ford himself has made to me since passing to the next stage of life (because all are direct quotes, I will omit the quotation marks):

Next year's election will return the Republicans to power, as they deserve to be, for the Democrats are split into a dozen warring factions and stand for nothing except to be against everything that Nixon tries to bring about. (I asked if this was definite or if conditions could change between now and the 1972 elections, and he replied) Nixon is a shoo-in. Bound to win. Agnew will be on the ticket.

Henry "Scoop" Jackson would be the best Democratic candidate, but he won't get the nomination.

164

We see Ted Kennedy as an active Presidential candidate but not successful at least for the next five years. Beyond that, events can be affected by what occurs between now and then.

Ethel Kennedy will not remarry for some time. Such a good mother! Too interested in her brood to risk their happiness with the type of avant garde man that she prefers.

The marriage of Jackie and Aristotle Onassis? Not such a bad one. They have more in common than she ever did with Jack Kennedy and his brothers and sisters. Both like money and power. Don't see it on the rocks for some time yet, and may be permanent.

Jordan will not much longer remain a separate nation. It will be gobbled up by Israel and Syria. A pity! A good king, Hussein.

Egypt will find itself a different form of government within the next ten years and will greatly profit by the changeover to a more monolithic form, but with greater freedom. This will come about when a strong man with good heart and head steps forward to assume power.

Turkey will remain strong and will not turn toward Communism, nor will Greece.

France will continue to be France—ups and downs and Gallic tears.

England remains strong but never reasserts her supremacy.

Vietnam? America will gradually withdraw from the arena of fighting, but the bloodshed will continue for a long time yet, without peace or sanity. When peace returns to Southeast Asia, the men who made up our fighting forces there will come home to severe unemployment and will not be able to adjust to the ways of the marketplace. They will need help with their problems, and the best way is through schools which teach psychological adjustment. America ought to begin planning now for work programs with veteran preferential to soak up the restlessness that will otherwise result. They aren't going to want to study as much as the World War II and Korean vets. These are activists, and they want to plunge right into careers or work.

Europe will not go Communist, and the Communist world will coexist with the so-called free for a long time to come. The hedonistic society of the Communist world will turn more and more toward God, because of these scientific mysteries (the psychic) which will more and more attract the attention of Soviet physicists and natural scientists. As they turn toward God, their minds and hearts will be opened and progress will be exceedingly rapid. Russia will turn more and more toward a freer society, and China will behave better when it gains admission to the United Nations.

Russia and China? Nothing serious on the horizon between them for at least fifteen years. No major war coming up there, just skirmishes and frictions. But the yellow and white races are going to be at each other's throats during the next decade, and what a pity, for all of us who have had many lifetimes in the flesh have been members of both races, and many more. The truth is that there is no such thing as race or color, but simply different souls which spring from the same source, God. Why, then, this bitterness between various races and creeds? The time will come after this century when lusts and hates are to be laid aside and peace for a long time shall reign on earth, but you will not live to see it in physical body.

Japan will rise to supremacy in the commercial mart and will boom the marketplaces with her cleverly designed wares but will not make trouble in a warlike way again in the foreseeable future, for the rest of the century.

Germany will slip a bit financially these next few years but will continue to be a power, with the two sectors somewhat closer together but not totally merged.

The Mexican economy will hold strong under good leadership. A fine place to invest now for the coming upturns.

Arab-Israeli problems are acute and will have to be

settled at the conference table before fighting gets out of hand, for that would set the civilized world back tens of thousands of years—the fratricidal slaying which takes us back to Cain and Abel. For a long time there will be disharmony in the Mideast, until at last Israel faces up to the terrible truth that it is not always right and others always wrong. They have been termed the Chosen People, but are they more chosen than those who themselves choose God? Israel is not what might be called a God-fearing nation in many respects today. The outward signs of worship, yes, but some of its leaders have turned away from God and will not always be victorious. It would be ridiculous to say that the Mideast crisis will pass until the hearts of men are uplifted. The smoldering fire remains until man himself alters his consciousness and overcomes hatred and greed. This present crisis will not, however, lead to violent confrontation by the entire world. No world war, but a continuing thorn in the flesh.

Cuba will gradually go down the drain with Castro. Then a new regime will negotiate with America and bring it back into the family of nations and the Organization of American States. We see this happening within the next four or five years.

Chile? An overthrow there before too long, and Communists no longer in power.

Central and South America? Communism is gaining ascendancy in some areas, as you know, and the strife will grow until a man of level-headed goodness comes to the helm in Argentina and Chile. Two similar types of men are due to take the helm in those countries within the next seven years.

A cancer cure? A start has already been made during the past year, and within the next seven years we will see a major breakthrough in finding that virus is part of the trigger but that man's attitudes and emotions play a vital part in the production of wild cells which are termed cancerous. Look for news from Germany on this score before too long.

Weather changes? Steadily increasing smog and contamination which automatically change weather by smokescreening earth from sun and moon. Hotter where it is hot and colder where it is cold, until the last decade of this century, when a major shift of the axis occurs and weather will be so drastically altered that it will be difficult to recognize former vegetations in various spots of the earth. Many people will not survive this shift, but others will, because after a period of churning seas and frightful wind velocities the turbulence will cease, and those in the north will live in a tropical clime, and vice versa. Before the year 2000 it will come to pass.

Will this shift be better or worse for the earth and its inhabitants? Six of one, half a dozen of the other. After the first frightened reaction, some people will settle down to their old pursuits, scheming how to capitalize to their own advantage on the cataclysmic event, while others will try to assuage the hardship of those who are adversely affected. The doers and the takers!

If this is bound to happen, why should we bother to try to correct environmental problems and worry about ecology? Why not be learning lessons now which will be invaluable for the future? Avoid repeating the same mistakes, and meanwhile hundreds of millions of people are breathing stale air and putrid fumes. What of the newborn babies, those returning souls who through no fault of their own find the air almost too contaminated to sustain life already?

Will California and Manhattan go into the sea before the end of the century? This eruption is overdue and will occur not too long hence, as Edgar Cayce predicted. Mexico will not be severely affected, except for the beach areas. The San Andreas fault in California is the first danger area, as it breaks apart and the land sinks into the sea. Manhattan somewhat later, as a sort of counter shift.

The peace for which man strives will elude him until shortly after the turn of the century, when peace suddenly stills the guns of war. This peace will not be because of a single man but because a race of pacifists who are being born in increasing numbers will suddenly gain sufficient control of the governments of the world to demand an end to the killings. These pacifists are those who so suffered during the Hundred Years War that they were willing to forgo further earth lives, until they saw the earth again plunged into almost constant slaughter in this century and are now determining to go into physical bodies to lead the cause of peace.

And on that more cheerful note, Arthur Ford ended his predictions.

# Epilogue

All of the material for this book was received during a four-month period beginning January 4, 1971, and concluding on May 7. At one of the final typing sessions I asked Arthur Ford if he would still be available at least until the book was published to answer queries, and he replied, "Won't be too far away, and Lily will be able to find me for you. Don't worry. We've always been on tap for each other, and I'm not going anyplace. Just working in a different sphere."

At our last session in May, Arthur wrote, "The task is about finished, and we are pleased with it and your faithfulness. I will now move on to other duties. Nor will Lily always be on hand, but if you wish to receive at this hour [8:30 A.M.] you will be protected by some of the group, and when you need Lily he will be here if the matter is urgent. We ask that before attempting the automatic writing you meditate and, as always, ask for protection, but we will not insist that you keep this up every morning. You need a rest now. Be a good girl, Ruth, and live according to that which we have written for this book. Love from all of us: Art, Lily, and the group. Go with God, amen."

The sadness of another parting! But not the desolate ache that I had experienced at news of his passing, for now I knew that he was joyously engaged in work that he loved in higher realms of consciousness. We would meet again, and meanwhile I too had work to do. The assignment that I am now completing has been an extraordinarily pleasant one. I had begun the manuscript in my usual manner, writing chapters in rough draft and then polishing before putting them into final form. But it soon became apparent that Arthur Ford's prose required so little editing that I wrote the remainder of the book on white bond paper, with inserted carbons.

As Lily had done in providing his material for *A Search for the Truth,* Arthur typed single-spaced on yellow paper, without punctuation or capitalization, but each sentence was perfectly formed. All that I omitted were apparently repetitious thoughts and messages of a purely personal nature having to do with myself or my family. Because spelling is not one of my strong points, I wasted considerable time checking questionable spelling in *Webster's Dictionary.* Invariably Arthur was right and I was wrong. His choice of words also drove me occasionally to the dictionary. He sometimes used the word "torpor," and I thought that he must have meant "stupor," but on checking I found that he had selected precisely the word that best expressed his meaning. He employed the expression "wont to do," and Webster verified that "wont" means accustomed. His word "centrifugal" threw me, but the dictionary defines its meaning as "proceeding away from the center; developing outward." Ford's personality shone forth on every page of his writing, and his good humor was never failing.

I would like to thank the many thousands of readers of my previous psychic books who have written to me concerning them. To spare others like trouble in writing, perhaps I should answer, in this remaining space, the questions most frequently asked.

"Can automatic writing be dangerous?" The answer is yes. Unless a person is well-balanced mentally and physically, he should not open a door through which mischievous or malevolent spirits can enter. As Arthur Ford wrote about a woman during a session in early April, "She is in no danger so long as she remains Christ-centered and lets her unconscious mind obey instructions from the guardian, or conscious mind. If she follows direction from the mind that ordinarily directs one's actions in that plane, she will come to no harm; but the moment that she begins to give free rein to the subconscious mind, she is in for trouble, for this is the mind where the memory bank is stored, and when it takes over as predominant it becomes a jumble of forgotten memories stored away in caves of the being, which should not all be unleashed at one time. Such a person, if the subconscious takes over, finds difficulty adjusting when she comes to this side of the open door. The subconscious mind thus liberated and turned loose seems to see and know all things but in actuality is without judgment or guidance. The poor woman may seem to be possessed by demons; for as Jesus cast forth demons from mad men beside the Sea of Galilee, He was actually reestablishing control of the conscious over the subconscious mind. It often takes many long years in earth time to restore balance between the conscious and subconscious minds. Let this be a warning to those in the physical body who ignore warnings about safety valves and time controls and other brakes to the free rein of the subconscious. They are unleashing all the nightmares of Pandora's box when they permit the subconscious to become the dominant mental state."

If you are intent on trying your hand at automatic writing, I strongly urge that you observe all the safety precautions I enumerated in *A Search for the Truth* and now repeat: Be sure that your intent is to seek spiritual growth, not frivolous amusement. Do not attempt it unless you are also meditating regularly each day for spiritual guidance. Always pray for protection before beginning automatic writing, and practice it no more than fifteen minutes each day, at exactly the same time, when your own guides are available. If evil entities come through, or foul language is used, give up the automatic writing instantly. You are not ready for spirit communication.

"Can you recommend a reliable medium, astrologist, or person who gives Cayce-type readings about past lives?" No, I am not sufficiently acquainted with professional psychics and cannot assume the responsibility of a recommendation.

"Is the Mr. A whom you wrote about in *A Search for the Truth* available to treat my ailments?" Unfortunately, Mr. A still insists upon anonymity, which is understandable, because I have received more than ten thousand requests for his services, and his own practice with magnetic healing was already overwhelming. Therefore, I do not have permission to divulge his identity.

"How can I safely develop my own psychic abilities or my awareness of past lives?" There are two nonprofit organizations which have study groups in various cities throughout the United States and Canada. These can be joined free or virtually without cost. Write to Spiritual Frontiers Fellowship (the group which Arthur Ford helped found) at 800 Custer Avenue, Evanston, Illinois 60202, or to the Association for Research and Enlightenment, P.O. Box 595, Virginia Beach, Virginia 23451, for information about joining or starting a group in your area. There is safety in numbers, even if only two or three meditate together. Both organizations have excellent psychic libraries, and members can borrow books from them by mail.

"Can you ask a question for me of your guides?" No. Lily has made plain that this is not their mission, and Arthur Ford has now gone on to other duties.

It is up to each of us to develop our own spiritual qualities through meditation, prayer, and the extension of a helping hand. No one else can forge the path for us. We must each find the way. And let us remember that the hardships and challenges of our lives help us to grow strong. We cannot always hope to have the wind at our backs.

# Glossary

Alpha body: The physical one.

Ashram: A habitat of yogis in the Orient, where psychic instruction is given to devotees.

Aum or Om: A spiritual chant used before meditation, which from the beginning of recorded history has been uttered in similar form by all races. The word "aum" represents God, and our word "amen" is thought to be a derivative of "aum."

Aura: A radiation said to surround all human bodies and capable of being seen by many psychics.

Automatic writing: The production of written messages, seemingly without the conscious thought of a living person, by means of a typewriter or a pencil held lightly on a piece of paper.

Beta body: The astral form which is said to surround the physical one and to be assumed at death.

Good Book: The Bible, which is replete with psychic experiences such as visions, discourse with the dead, prophecy, spiritual healing, discerning spirits, automatic writing, and extrasensory perception.

Karma: The law of cause and effect—the Biblical "eye for an eye," meaning that what we do to others will be done to us.

Mantram: The Sanskrit name for the one or more

syllables intoned at the beginning of a meditation. Each person is said to have a different mantram which represents his unique vibration with the Universal One.

Medium: A psychic person through whom communication is apparently made between the living and dead.

Psychometrist: One who can psychically perceive facts concerning an object or its owner solely by personal contact with the object.

Reincarnation: The belief that each soul returns again and again to physical body in order to atone for past errors and seek perfection. Reincarnation is not to be confused with transmigration of souls into animal forms, a belief held by some Eastern sects.

Séance or Sitting: A gathering of people to seek communication with the spirit world through a medium.

Spirit Control: A discarnate (like Fletcher) who seemingly relays messages from souls beyond the grave to living people through a medium.

Spirit Guide: A discarnate who seems to write or speak through a living person.

Trance: A state in which the conscious mind rests while another entity presumably takes over.